Exercising
muscles and minds

Outdoor play and the early years curriculum

Marjorie Ouvry

national
children's
bureau

Published by the National Children's Bureau, Registered Charity number 258825. 8 Wakley Street, London EC1V 7QE. Tel: 020 7843 6000. Website: www.ncb.org.uk

© National Children's Bureau, 2003

Published 2003, reprinted 2005

ISBN 1 904787 01 0

British Library Cataloguing in Publication Data
A catalogue record for this book is available from the British Library

Acknowledgements

This book is entirely influenced by the inspiration and challenge I have received from the children, staff, colleagues, students, practitioners and parents with whom I have worked during my career. My editor, Pat Gordon Smith of the National Early Years Network, asked me to write this book in the first place and I am grateful for her help and constant encouragement. Thanks to Thelma Miller and her wonderful staff at Clyde Nursery School, to Judy Stevenson and Greenwich Nursery School Heads, to Thelma Perkins, to Heather Shannon of the Jesmond Nursery in Newcastle and to Rie Madsen of the Forest School in Odense, Denmark for sharing ideas with me. I was continually refreshed by exciting examples of good practice from the many practitioners on in-service courses which I ran, particularly those in Haringey. Many lent me excellent photographs of children outdoors, which it has sadly been impossible to include in this book. Thanks to Celia Burgess-Macey who read a very early draft and made such helpful suggestions on multicultural and gender issues. Finally, thanks to Jonathan, whose practical support (dish and clothes washing, ironing and shopping) and literacy support (reading and commenting on the text) have been invaluable.

Contents

Introduction

Margaret McMillan, pioneer of nursery education, campaigned early in the 20th century for young children to be educated in a distinct learning environment centred around the nursery garden. As early as 1919, she described the passivity and poor diet of children.

Children are malnourished, eat the wrong things at the wrong intervals. Life for many children is so inert and so unwholesome that they do not digest well. This is true of many well cared for children behind model dishes in model schools as well as the poor and neglected. They sit about. They are over-clothed. They do not run and shout in the open. They sleep in stuffy air.[1]

It seems extraordinary that McMillan, writing about children in the early 20th century, should hit such a modern note. And it is because the children she describes have so much in common with our children today that it is helpful to look at what she did. McMillan wanted every child to benefit from the conditions she had seen for well-to-do children when she had been their governess.

The ideal of such buildings [nurseries] should be home life, not school life as we know it; that is what is required for the children of wealth. It is needed for the children of all classes.[2]

Margaret McMillan opened her model nursery school in Deptford in southeast London to show the world the successful design of a nursery school in a garden, with children flowing freely between inside and out. The focus of the school was the garden planned for children's learning: 'The best classroom and the richest cupboard is roofed only by the sky.'[3] It is thanks to Margaret McMillan that there is an emphasis on the outdoor environment in the nursery education tradition, and it is an important legacy which McMillan has bequeathed to us.[4]

I began my teaching career in the 1960s in the northeast of Scotland, where the weather is far from hospitable. Even so, there was an expectation that children would have access to outdoor play every day, all year round. The early years inspector regularly asked nursery teachers to fill in a form notifying her of days when we had not managed to allow the children out, and the reasons why not. Woe betide us if our reasons were not good enough!

Twenty years later, I became head of the Rachel McMillan Nursery School, which was established by Margaret McMillan and named after her sister. Not surprisingly, for an institution founded by Margaret McMillan, the belief that a well-planned outdoor environment answers children's learning needs was central to the school.

By the time I was appointed head, I was steeped in the conviction that access to outdoor play at all times of the year is a crucial part of children's learning and all-round development. Now, the importance of outdoor play has been recognised by the Qualifications and Curriculum Authority in its good practice guidelines for the early learning goals, which repeatedly stress that young children should have access to a well-planned outdoor area (see box opposite). It is a tremendous breakthrough that young children's entitlement to outdoor play has been officially endorsed – but having the space is just the beginning; knowing how to use it is the next step.

My motivation for writing *Exercising muscles and minds* comes from the wonderful learning that I have observed out of doors in many under-fives settings up and down the country, and I wish to offer the benefit of those observations to practitioners and the children with whom they work. To help achieve that, the book sets out the reasons why there are more opportunities for children to learn when they have access to an outdoor space. It informs practitioners about their role in bringing all the learning goals into the outdoors, where freedom of movement is the key to quality learning and where children can feel secure, relaxed and open to new experiences. The book is deliberately practical, with inexpensive and imaginative ideas that can be used in any setting, however unpromising the outdoor premises may seem. It is possible to create stimulating places and situations from extremely simple things, and many of the ideas found here require little or no money because they use nature, natural materials and the elements. However, all of them require commitment and imagination.

Exercising muscles and minds focuses on outdoor play and learning for the Foundation Stage, so looks mainly at work with children aged three to five. The purpose of this book is to:

- question the assumptions about the value of outdoor learning;
- strengthen the conviction that learning outside is of equal status with learning indoors and that, for many children, it is more important;
- refresh those who want to hear again the reasons why access to an outdoor environment is so important;
- help those who want to organise their outdoor area and make it an available and stimulating learning space;
- show some patterns of planning for practitioners to compare with their own;
- share practical, economic (often free) and simple ideas to support the curriculum;

QCA curriculum guidance

Well-planned play, both indoors and outdoors, is a key way in which young children learn with enjoyment and challenge. In playing, they behave in different ways: sometimes their play will be boisterous, sometimes they will describe and discuss what they are doing, sometimes they will be quiet and reflective as they play.

The role of the practitioner is crucial in:

- planning and resourcing a challenging environment;
- supporting children's learning through planned play activity;
- extending and supporting children's spontaneous play; and
- extending and developing children's language and communication in their play.

Through play, in a secure environment with effective adult support, children can:

- explore, develop and represent learning experiences that help them make sense of the world;
- practise and build up ideas, concepts and skills;
- learn how to control impulses and understand the need for rules;
- be alone, be alongside others or cooperate as they talk or rehearse their feelings;
- take risks and make mistakes;
- think creatively and imaginatively;
- communicate with others as they investigate or solve problems;
- express fears or relive anxious experiences in controlled and safe situations.[5]

- encourage practitioners to interact with children outside, not as supervisors but as educators;
- help practitioners inform parents and others about the importance of outdoor learning for their children; and
- encourage staff teams to draw up outdoor play policies.

The outdoor environment holds all that is of value to the growing and learning child. I urge practitioners to be bold and imaginative in helping children to learn outdoors, and hope this book will provide them with the inspiration and practical ideas with which to do so.

1 Girls and boys come OUT to play

Why play?

Children experience the world through sight, sound, touch, taste and smell. At the same time as their senses are processing the experience, their feelings about the experience are fixed in their memory. Finding ways of teaching very young children that are going to result in positive feelings is one of the most important jobs we have as early years educators. An inappropriate approach can engender feelings of inadequacy, failure or fear, while an appropriate method can give the children tremendous confidence in themselves as learners.

Play has long been recognised as the key way in which children come to make their own sense of their often confusing world. Playing allows children to invent their own rules, to integrate the past with the present, to recreate the present and rehearse the future. It is such a motivating force that it has always been used by skilful and sensitive adults in the educational process as a powerful means to helping children stay positive about learning. Play provides a rich method for children to express what they know and, most significantly, how they feel about the world and their relationships.

The value of play in childhood is very succinctly expressed by the Cambridge University biologist Patrick Bateson:

Children are not miniature adults. Some of their behaviour is like scaffolding – a specialised structure used in building the adult, which loses its use once this task is completed. Play is an important example of such developmental scaffolding, and without it the adult is more difficult to build.[6]

It is common for adults to look at children who are left to their own devices and say: 'Look, the children are playing'. But, in fact, they may not be playing. They might be exploring with their senses:

- What is it?
- What does it feel, look, smell, taste like?
- Where have I seen something like this before?
- What is it for?
- What can I do with it?

Play happens when children bring their individual knowledge totally under their own control and 'pretend'. So children do not play all the time. However, what they must have in order to benefit from play is long periods of time in a well-planned play-based environment. Given the right context for play, they can slip in and out of play easily,

The benefits of play

The *Quality in diversity* framework found a new way of describing the benefits of play in children's learning:

Belonging and connecting in play
By their play, children are learning about each other, and about how people live, work and play together, in families and many other kinds of groups. They are exploring cultural differences. they are learning about different kinds of relationships, which they repeat, renew and recreate in their imaginative play.

Being and becoming in play
By their play, children are learning about themselves, about who they are and what they might become. They experiment with what they can do without fear of failure. They develop confidence, a sense of self-worth and identity. They make and break their own rules. They try out different roles, explore and challenge stereotypes. They learn to communicate with increasing skill and confidence.

Contributing and participating in play
By their play, children are learning to take risks and to be responsible for their actions. In cooperative play they begin to accept responsibility for others. They learn to persevere, and gain satisfaction from joining with others.

Being active and expressive in play
By their play, children explore and transform their worlds. They talk about their discoveries, sharing them with children and adults. They are learning to act like scientists, musicians and artists, curiously trying out new possibilities, finding new ways of expressing their ideas and their interests, their identities and their membership of diverse family and cultural groups.

Thinking, imagining and understanding in play
By their play, children use their imagination to explore ideas and feelings. They are learning to make sense of their own experiences, to learn from the experiences of others. In their play, children puzzle and dream, create stories and imaginary worlds. They have space and time to wonder at the world about them, and to struggle with and reflect on deep feelings and challenge ideas, and develop a sense of fairness and justice.[7]

testing out their ideas and making sense of them. They talk about real things, they experience real things and how real people behave, and then they represent real and imagined things, people and situations in their play. For this flowing between the real and imagined, children need space to move and freedom to move.

Why play out of doors?

David and Obe have been on a visit with their nursery to the fire station where they climbed into the engine, held the powerful hoses and squirted water over the ground.

Back in the nursery outdoor space, staff have provided hoses and hard hats and there is a little KOMPAN house which the two children imagine to be on fire. They make noises of the water rushing through the hose and of the fire engine's siren, they shout 'fire, fire – get out of the house – you'll be burned' and rush around in great excitement spraying imaginary water on the roof of the house.

David and Obe were given the exciting first-hand experience of visiting the fire station and were then helped by their educators to make sense of it. Provision was made for them to recall, record and make connections with their existing knowledge in the most effective way – through imaginative play. Older primary school children might have been asked to recall that same experience through more sedentary tasks such as whole-class discussion, drawing a poster about the dangers of fire or creating an advertising slogan for joining the fire service. The most effective way that young children recall and record their experiences is through playing out the experience dramatically.

Let's imagine what might have happened if David and Obe had stayed indoors after their visit. Back at the nursery they might have taken a cardboard tube from the junk area and 'transformed' it into a hose. The excited children may then have rushed around 'putting out fires' and making fire-play sounds. But would the nursery staff have found their play appropriate for indoors – especially if they have worked hard to establish with the children that it can be dangerous to run around inside and that different levels of noise apply inside and out? Rather than allowing the children to express themselves fully, as they would have done outside, staff may reasonably end up saying: 'Remember, little voices inside!' or 'Take care, you might bang into someone if you run around like that'. And these active children would basically be receiving the message: 'Be quiet! Don't move!'

Outdoor space, even if it is only a small area, allows and encourages children to relive their experiences through their most natural channel: movement. The opportunity for movement is therefore a very significant reason for giving young children access to the outside, and is given here as the first of six good reasons why playing outdoors should be an essential part of every child's daily experience.

1 | Movement

Information about the world

Right from birth there is such a powerful urge to move that babies soon struggle to be freed from the constraints of adult arms or restricting buggies, and will bounce their legs up and down in continual mock walking movements when lying on the floor or sitting in a car seat. Older babies begin to crawl, and the pleasure of quickly discovering things near and far, hard and soft, under and over, can even delay the progress to standing and walking. 'He didn't need to walk because he could crawl so fast and efficiently,' said one young mother describing her zoomy offspring.

Young children learn about themselves and their environment through movement. Jean Piaget, Jerome Bruner and Margaret Donaldson – great and influential developmental psychologists – say that for our youngest children, movement is 'thought in action'. Children have first to experience the world actively through all their senses before they can think in the abstract and hold thoughts or the memory of those things in their heads as pictures, concepts or symbols.

Context for role play

From the age of about two, children begin to use less realistic objects in their play and can pretend, for example, that a block is a telephone. Before that age they usually need an actual cup to offer the pretend tea. Later, they can even imagine situations and pretend to be characters that they have experienced in real life, in books or on the television without any object to help them. This is role play.

However, children need enough space to make their role play believable to them. The outside area can provide this all-important space that sustains their play and enables adults to join in. Children in group settings need to be able to role play outside every day, with support from objects, or props, for playing out their ideas in big enough spaces. It is not nearly so satisfying to push your 'baby' in its buggy a few steps from the home corner to the book corner as it is to go for a proper walk.

The chance to express emotions

When we are feeling grumpy, the poet Kipling exhorts us to 'take a large hoe and a shovel also and dig 'til you gently perspire'.[8]

I was watching a group of children playing imaginatively and (loudly) on a climbing frame when one child left the group and stomped off for about ten metres in an exaggerated huff. Something had clearly upset him and he was able to translate that setback into movement. After a few minutes, he returned to the group in a better frame of mind. He had had the space to move away from the cause of his trouble, reflect on it, calm down and return without loss of dignity.

In the outside space, children can also run and jump for joy, or squeal with glee and excitement, as well as stamp with anger.

Activity and development

Education policy in England and Wales is currently focused on getting children to read and write as young as possible. Whatever your view on this, it is clear that children must have built, coordinated and controlled the muscles in their arms and hands before they are able to hold a pencil and manipulate it. (A few moments trying to write with the hand you don't usually use gives a good approximation of the muscle strength and control needed by children who are learning to write. It will not be long before the muscles in your forearm begin to ache. What better way to put children off writing than to give them a task that will make their arms hurt!) Children can strengthen the muscles and refine their motor skills if they are given the chance to climb, push and pull heavy things around, and to swing – all of which they tend to do naturally when they play and explore their surroundings.

While the children benefit from the freedom to practise their motor skills, practitioners benefit from opportunities to identify those skills in the children with whom they work, to help them be aware of their growing competence and to teach new skills.

Growth and development of the brain, body and feelings are inseparable. At the same time as children are gaining control over their muscles, their minds are being exercised as feelings about themselves and their abilities are established. Piaget saw movement and physical development as the prerequisite for higher levels of thinking. Other research stresses the importance of movement and gross motor play for intellectual development.[9]

Regular physical activity in the early years helps to set a pattern of fitness for the rest of life. There are many worrying studies informing us that young children are less fit now than is good for them. For example, in a recent study 98% of ten-year-old girls were found to be unfit, and 95% of boys of the same age.[10] Fatty foods and a sedentary lifestyle of television and computer viewing have led children into being couch potatoes instead of runner beans.

A recent study indicates that the potential for heart disease later in life begins in early childhood and that this potential can be triggered by lack of adequate exercise when very young.[11]

2 | The right to space all year round

If movement is such an important aspect of a child's development, access to space must be part of a daily routine in order to nurture this mind–body growth. Going outside to explore and play cannot be perceived as something that is suitable only in the summer. Children need to be given access to the outdoors all year long.

Chapter 3 looks into the difficulties that some settings face in offering children an outdoor space and how to tackle them – and tackle them we must. Margaret McMillan, the early pioneer of nursery education, said:

> Children want space at all ages. But from the age of one to seven, space, that is ample space, is almost as much wanted as food and air. To move, to run, to find things out by new movement, to feel one's life in every limb, that is the life of early childhood. And yet one sees dim houses behind whose windows and doors thirty to forty little ones are penned in Day Nurseries.[12]

If we substitute the term 'reception classes' for 'Day Nurseries', we may wonder what has changed in 70 years.

When children are denied adequate space they often feel desperately frustrated and this can lead to uncooperative behaviour. If children are cramped at home *and* at nursery or reception class, they may be denied the kind of learning and development that can only be gained in the freedom of outdoor spaces.

In Haringey, a nursery nurse recently changed her practice, enabling the children to have indoor–outdoor access whenever they want it. She described the difference:

> Before we changed our practice, the children had a brief run around before lunch outside, but only if the weather was deemed to be fine and warm. The children were like pressure cookers; I could feel the tension building up, especially among some boys, as the time for going out approached. When the doors were opened they would explode into the outside area.
>
> I can't believe how calm they all are now that there is free access. Everyone – parents and staff – has remarked on the improvement in the children's behaviour and level of concentration, both indoors and out.

3 | The need for risky freedom

There is a growing perception that walking anywhere is dangerous. It seems safer to go by car. Of course parents want their children to be 'safe' and free from mortal danger, but our perception of the situations that pose a threat to children's safety does not necessarily reflect reality. Traffic is certainly a cause for real concern, as cars are driven increasingly fast in residential streets and the number of vehicles on the roads continues to climb. But strangers pose no more of a threat to young children than they did 30 years ago, when we considered ourselves to be living in a safer world. The risk of a child being killed or abducted by a stranger in the UK is less that one in a million and the incidence actually fell in the 1990s. Sensationalist reports in the newspapers and on television have given parents the perception that their children are in jeopardy all the time, leading to the trend towards planning and supervising children's time too rigorously and restricting their free time. So, a young child might attend a nursery or reception class whose approach dictates tasks defined by an adult all day, only to be driven off afterwards to highly structured gym, swimming or ballet class.

In this heavily structured world, when are children to play and socialise freely, and to use their own imagination and initiative? Children find out about themselves and their own abilities during free play, while too much cosseting can prevent them from developing that knowledge and establishing self-confidence. Being busy all day can mean a programme of adult-directed activities that limit the freedom which outdoor play allows.

For a full discussion of how to safeguard children from real threats to their safety while giving them the freedom to make their own decisions and experiment with their limits, see Jennie Lindon's book, *Too safe for their own good?*[13]

4 | Unique opportunities for learning

Some opportunities for learning can only happen outside. The experience of a change in the weather, finding a colony of ants under a big stone, making a large-scale construction with huge cardboard cartons or painting on great long strips of wallpaper – all of these motivate children into mental and physical engagement, and can only be done outside. Children begin to notice the movement of shadows or the process of evaporation, and skilled practitioners can joke with them to stimulate interest in further study, for example: 'Who pinched that puddle? There was definitely one here this morning and now it's gone.' In fact all the learning goals can be achieved outside while the children's health and wellbeing are also being boosted. Outside, children can run fast – even in small outdoor areas. They can shout and squeal and find out what their bodies and voices can really do. And all of this can be tied up to measurable learning.

5 | Improved behaviour

When I was a headteacher I was frequently asked to admit, as a priority, children from cramped home conditions who were driving their distressed parents mad by their incessant activity. They were labelled 'hyperactive'. These children knew instinctively that they needed space in which to move and had been trying to let people know in the only way they could – by showing it in their behaviour. As soon as they came to nursery they calmed down at home. The nursery had no magic powers, only access for long periods to an outdoor area where adults supported all areas of their learning through allowing them to play freely and to move about.

High activity levels and disruptive behaviour are not generally signs of behavioural problems in young children, but are normal and typical for pre-school children who are just beginning to bring action under the control of thought. However, research has shown that in environments that enable children to move about, to collaborate with others and take frequent breaks during sedentary activities, the behaviour of children who have a tendency to lose their temper or get over-excited is less disturbing.[14]

Studies in the United States suggest that one in eighteen children is being diagnosed as having Attention Deficit Hyperactivity Disorder (ADHD) and half that number is being given Ritalin. In Britain, too, the prescribing of this drug is on the increase. Ritalin suppresses children's desire to be active and, as a result, they conform to the sedentary tasks set out at school. This makes the teachers' job much easier and in many cases helps older children to settle down. However, developmental psychologists are highly concerned about the drug being given to young children. The long-term consequences on the child's all-round development are unknown, but the main concern is that a drug is being used specifically to eradicate a characteristic of early childhood; children are being perceived as problems for being active.

Is it possible that some young children are being diagnosed as hyperactive simply because there aren't enough places for them to play and move freely? If so, it would make the case even stronger for those children to have access to as much outdoor play as possible – for the sake of their long-term social, emotional and mental health.

6 | Serving the needs of young boys

Most people who work with young children would say that boys and girls play differently and are attracted to different activities. Boys are generally more interested in action, exploration and the vigorous fantasy play associated with superheroes (all interests which require a lot of space for movement) whereas girls, stereotypically, like playing imaginatively in the home corner and working with and alongside adults. Girls come to an understanding of the adult world through domestic play and talk; they use 'reading' and 'writing' in their play because their brains are more developed for language at the three- to five-year-old stage. Of course, these differences between boys and girls can be exaggerated if they are accepted unquestioningly ('boys will be boys'), and care needs to be taken that adult assumptions do not block opportunities for all children.

Most of the adults who work with our youngest children are women, and they tend to feel more comfortable with the talkative and compliant girls. It is not uncommon to visit early years settings where a female staff member is sitting surrounded by a group of accommodating, talkative little girls. At the same time the boys' seemingly chaotic and boisterous play is either ignored ('I can't handle that') or interrupted ('What is going on here – you're making far too much noise'), probably because practitioners fear it is getting out of control.

Some practitioners spend a great deal of effort trying to attract boys into areas of interest that have been traditionally thought of as belonging to girls, and vice versa. But young boys' brains mature in a different sequence to those of young girls and, in some areas, at a slower rate. Boys first develop the parts of the brain for knowing about movement and the space in which they have to move themselves and other things. They are not so interested in language or how other people operate, yet this aspect fascinates some girls. Some practitioners go with the flow and accept the differing developmental pace. They start to enter the child's world and skilfully play with and alongside his or her interests. Other areas of the curriculum then arise meaningfully out of the play.

On the whole, pre-schools and nurseries, as well as schools, emphasise sedentary activities that focus on children who are good at talking, fitting in, cottoning on quickly and understanding other people's (especially the teacher's) intentions. Active boys can begin to feel uncomfortable in such settings because they generally seem to feel more secure in the outdoor environment. By giving less attention to the outdoor environment and the quality of outdoor play, we may be denying access to education to a significant number of boys – and it is possible that the seeds of boys' under-achievement in education are sown in these early years.[15]

An essential teaching area

The outdoor space must be viewed as an essential teaching and learning environment which is linked with the learning that goes on inside, but with even greater status because it allows for children to learn through movement.

Children recognise their own need to move about. In a recent piece of research, young children were asked what they liked best about nursery. Overwhelmingly it was being outside.

When it comes to play children were most enthusiastic about playing out of doors. We gave the children Polaroid cameras and asked them to record what they liked most about nursery. One little boy took a picture of a crawl-through tunnel and another photographed a football. They really valued the open space, especially if there were things like climbing frames and bikes. It's interesting because a lot of people who look after children probably prefer spending time with them indoors.[16]

As early years practitioners, if we believe that young children learn through play – that play is thought in action – then offering children a playing space outdoors would seem the most efficient means to fulfil their need to play, learn through first-hand experiences and cooperate with others.

2 So why do the girls and boys stay IN?

The last chapter put forward several compelling reasons for why children should have access to an outdoor area. But practitioners often provide what seem to be equally compelling reasons for *not* going

---

Practitioners said ...
'It's too dangerous out of doors. Parents want us to keep their children safe.'
'It's too cold / wet / windy / hot.'
'We don't have direct access to the outdoor area and getting out is such a major upheaval that we only do it in the sunny summer days.'
'As a Year 1 teacher, I need children who have learnt to sit down for the literacy and numeracy hours.'
'It's boring outside.'
'Some children would spend all day outside! We'd never get them in.'
'We don't have enough space.'

A child said ...
'My mum says I've not to go out again because I get too muddy.'

Headteachers said ...
'They don't learn outdoors they just run around.'
'There is too much space to supervise and too few staff.'

Parents said ...
'Don't let him go out today because he's got a cold.'
'Outside their clothes get dirty, muddy, wet.'
'I want him inside, sitting down and learning.'

An inspector said ...
'How can you possibly cover the curriculum if you are outside all the time?'

---

outside. In the box are some of the reasons I have heard from practitioners, parents, inspectors and even children.

The reasons given in the box for not using the outdoors can be grouped into general categories of concerns about:

- safety and staffing;
- curriculum and learning;
- behaviour;
- the weather;
- health; and
- the difficulties of the building.

All these reasons for not going outside are genuinely felt and, in some cases, there might be real difficulties attached to getting out of doors – for instance, if the setting is on the first floor of a building with no direct access to outside. When staff in any setting give reasons for not taking the children outside every day, they have the children's best interests at heart, but often show a lack of understanding about the full potential of the available outdoor area in terms of children's learning and motivation. Many of the reasons are based on fears and anxieties rather than on knowledge of children's needs. What assumptions are they making about outdoor play which lead to their reasons for staying inside?

Assumption 1: 'Outside is dangerous'

The outside area is a place in which, as practitioners, we want children to move and to be physically active – which means they are more likely to fall and hurt themselves than if they are sitting down inside. How can these two features of outside learning be reconciled? Perhaps we should question our own discomfort about children and safety. Yes, it is risky, but in playing outside children can test out what their bodies are capable of while seeing what their friends can do. Being at the edge of what they can manage is where learning happens. It is when the environment that we set up for children enables them to be adventurous and show physical and social courage that children can begin to understand themselves and others.

Is the outside really more dangerous?

In June 1999, I conducted a survey of three nursery schools with 300 children between them and a staff ratio of 1:13 (all staff members were either teachers or nursery nurses). During the whole month, just 16 reportable accidents were found to have occurred in the outdoor areas. They were all minor accidents. Falls from a trike or apparatus, tripping while running and the like resulted in grazed knees, minor cuts and bruises. During the survey, one headteacher said:

> Most accidents outside are minor cuts and bruises. The things that give rise to them are not 'dangerous' – falling when running and similar things. A pencil in an eye – whether indoors or out – is potentially far more dangerous, but we don't suggest banning pencils.

The kind of accidents that happen outside occur because there is space to move quickly. Children get bumps, but they have hard-boned areas – the skull, knee caps and shins – as protection. Similar accidents happen in soft rooms inside too.

Limiting outdoor playtime does not help children to behave well. Young children can waste time hanging around waiting for the moment they will be allowed outdoors, asking 'Is it time to go outside yet?' In these circumstances, when the doors eventually open there is an excited rush so that accidents and quarrels are more likely to happen.

When children are given the choice of being indoors or out, they know that the outdoors is not a scarce and rationed commodity. They know they can go outside when they feel the need to be active and remain there for enough time to finish their game. They also know that they can be indoors when they wish and that they will not be forced to go out in the middle of an inside activity. (See Chapter 3 and Chapter 7 for information about managing and planning for free choice.) If it is not possible to give the children free choice about whether they want to be indoors or out, have a stated policy about how they can use the outdoors every day and let all the children know when outdoor play happens during the day (see Chapter 8). If possible, give the children direct access to the outdoor area from the playroom. (See Chapter 3 for ideas about what to do when the setting does not have direct access.)

Outdoor 'risk' and disabled children

Because the outdoor area is perceived to be more dangerous than inside, disabled children are sometimes over-protected and needlessly kept inside. A stimulating well-planned outdoor learning environment is beneficial for all children, and disabled children are entitled to the same chance to be independent learners as all other children. A child with mobility problems, for example, needs opportunities to strengthen their limbs by taking physical and social risks outside at their own pace and ability.

Practitioners need to support individual achievement without comparing children's attainment. This approach will enable children with disabilities to value their own physical success and the effort involved, and counter low aspirations which may hinder the physical development which is so crucial to all other aspects of their learning.

The outdoor environment can be the key factor to motivate learning for disabled children and can be adapted for use by (and to the advantage of) all the children. For example, in one nursery a ramp was made specifically to be used by one child in a wheelchair. This enabled other children to push their carts or carry articles of different weight up a gradient and to discover the extra effort required. It also added to their fun.

Assumption 2: 'Higher adult:child ratios are needed outside'

Practitioners often feel that more members of staff are needed to supervise outdoor play than indoor play. I have heard this argument used by practitioners from all types of settings, whether they have a ratio of 1:13, 1:8 or 1:6. For example, an early years worker remarked that she would be able to give the children the opportunity of in/out access if only she had a ratio of 1:6, yet another setting offers children the free in/out experience with ratios of 1:13. The ratio is not really the issue, it is the knowledge and confidence of the staff and whether they believe that children really do need outdoor access. However, in most cases, practitioners seem happy with the existing ratio for working indoors with the children.

It is possible that, if staff believe the outside to be more risky, they might fear they will be blamed if there were to be an accident. But if we accept that Assumption 1 is *not* true – that children are not really more at risk outside than they are indoors – then staff do not really have anything more than usual to fear from allowing the children to play out of doors.

Assumption 3: 'Educators are merely supervisors outdoors'

This is a very serious assumption as it can lead to the denial of vital aspects of good professional practice which practitioners have worked hard to build up indoors. For example, practitioners who feel they are simply supervisors when outdoors may fail to interact with the children as they play and may not extend the children's interests in ways that they always would inside.

Role of adult

Children are wonderful observers and take their cue from the adults' behaviour. If they see an adult who is apparently doing nothing outside except warning children to 'be careful' and sorting out fights, they may conclude that adults are not interested in their outdoor learning and may therefore see it as a less worthwhile area themselves.

Chapter 7 discusses the importance of practitioners knowing their role in the outdoor area in order to help the children continue learning outside, and to achieve job satisfaction for themselves.

Assumption 4: 'No learning happens outside'

Frequent lack of attention to the external environment probably comes from some bizarre assumption that knowledge acquired indoors is superior to that gained outside.[17]

Many practitioners have an unconscious belief that effective learning only happens when children are still, quiet and calm, with pencil and paper to hand and with a teacher nearby to offer instruction. The flipside of this belief is the idea that when children are physically active they can't be learning anything to do with the curriculum. These views are often based on little more than practitioners' own learning experiences, especially if they have not had the opportunity to reflect on what is meant by 'learning' in early education.

What young children learn when sitting still

The most advanced level of movement is the ability to stay totally still, which requires entire muscle groups to work in cooperation with balance and posture. Children who are unable to sit still or pay attention need more time engaged in physical activities if they are to gain full control over involuntary movements and so develop the skills needed to control voluntary actions.[18]

The ways in which very young children access knowledge are complex because the growth of mind and body is inseparable. This means that children are learning many things all at the same time. So, if a 20-minute circle time fails to capture children's individual interests they may learn nothing from it, except that this daily session is where they are made to 'sit still' – a boring and uncomfortable lesson. I heard of one wonderfully insightful child who, during a long 'carpet' session, suddenly announced: 'I'm too young for this; I'm going outside to play.' And off he went. Sadly, assertive children like this are all too few. Most comply with inappropriately set tasks to please their teacher. Children can sit still and pay attention for long periods when in the grip of their chosen interest. Equally they can concentrate and persevere for long periods when dancing and climbing.

After observing the 'carpet' and group time of the literacy hour in a Year 1 class, a teacher of the Alexander Technique concluded:

The patterns of (postural) misuse learned when they are young, eg pulling the head and neck down, collapsing in the spine, hunching in the shoulders, gripping the pencil, could stay with them for the rest of their lives and could lead to serious back problems in later life.[19]

The need to plan for outdoor learning

It is certainly true that if the outdoors is not well planned and the setting does not have clear aims for children's learning outside, then practitioners may find it difficult to see any worthwhile learning going on outside. But this is true when considering any environment for young children – inside or out.

Without clarity of aims and learning intentions for children in play situations it is impossible to know what to look for when observing the children or to know how to further the children's learning. Structuring the environment and supporting children's learning is as important outside as in.

Assumption 5: 'We would go outside more if the weather were better'

This assumption may appear to grow out of a concern for children who might not want to be out in cold, wet or windy weather – though in reality it is generally practitioners who don't want to be out in it. When encouraged to enjoy all sorts of weather, most children love the experience of the elements and can be highly motivated into asking questions and furthering their lines of enquiry (see pp. 70–75 for activities that can be used in all sorts of weathers).

> The weather – well this is one of our most valuable resources. Sun, rain, snow, mist, wind ... all provide experiences which can increase children's knowledge and understanding of the world in which they live. Taking a positive approach, a collection of wellingtons can help avoid potential problems when rain or snow leave puddles and muddy patches. Umbrellas for 'rainy walks' can alleviate the 'pain' of very wet days when equipment can't be set up outside. Warm coats, gloves and boots will ensure that staff as well as children feel comfortable on cold days. Once adults have taken the decision to treat the indoor and outdoor areas as one, then the odd occasion that children can't go out will be far outnumbered by the times children enjoy continuous free movement between the areas.[20]

Even where children have direct access to the outdoors, the weather sometimes deters practitioners if the door needs to be kept open for freedom of access as this can make the inside too cold in winter. Some nurseries have solved this by investing in an inexpensive slow-closing device on the door. In cold or windy weather, the door needn't be left open, but the children can still operate it without slamming it shut.

While encouraging children to be outside, it is important to ensure that precautions are taken to ensure that they do not burn in hot sun. Some nurseries have a store of sun hats and long-sleeved T-shirts, while others create sheltered areas.

Assumption 6: 'It's more healthy to be inside than out'

Parents sometimes ask staff to keep their children inside because they might catch a cold. But a cold is a virus; something that is passed from one person to another – and with much greater ease when people are sitting close together indoors than when they are moving about outside. There is no evidence to show that children can catch a cold from being in the fresh air, exercising, becoming interested in some creature they have found or playing a ring game with an adult, whatever the common belief might be. However, children do need to be suitably clothed whatever the weather, and if they are not feeling well they are probably better kept comfortable, warm, quiet and with an adult who will keep them snug.

Some people worry that there is more pollution outside in inner city play areas than in the classrooms. But it is the same air in the classrooms. Given that all the air is polluted, at least children are on the move when they are outside, filling and emptying their lungs with new air rather than breathing in air that is continually circulating around their classrooms – air that is much more likely to generate coughs and infection.

Another assumption to do with health is the worry of many parents that their child's asthma might get worse by being active and being out of breath through running. The only thing that can be certain about asthma is that children experience it differently, so the amount of activity an asthmatic child takes on must be managed carefully, in consultation with the child's parents. In some cases, activity may be the key to helping asthmatic children strengthen their lungs and build up their immune system. Asthma experts advise children to use their inhaler before strenuous exercise, and asthmatic children's inhalers should therefore be available to them whenever they need them.

It is important to remember that some disabled children are vulnerable to chest infections and complications. They can go outside and get wet, but should not *stay* wet. Also, poor circulation can mean that they will get colder than other children (immobility can mean very cold extremities), so might need wrapping up more warmly. Some children with health problems such as sickle cell anaemia should be kept warm at all times. Practitioners can work with parents to devise creative solutions to ensure that the entitlement to activity and the outdoor curriculum is not suspended because of one aspect of the child's health.

Assumption 7: 'Parents don't like the children being outside'

As mentioned in Chapter 1, the development of physical and mental skills in young children is closely linked (see pp. 11–14), so the skills they develop while playing in a well-planned outdoor area contribute to their all-round growth into avid readers, enthusiastic writers, problem solvers and cooperative friends. Parents are concerned that their children learn and develop well. It is therefore important that early years practitioners show parents how free movement outside actually contributes to their children's learning. See Chapter 9 for ways to inform parents.

Assumption 8: 'Getting out is such an upheaval, we can only do it on sunny days'

Many settings have a genuine problem with getting access to outdoor space, and it would be unfair to suggest that there is a simple solution to this. However, the fact that getting out is problematic needn't – and shouldn't – mean that children are denied access to the open air. The next chapter provides some suggestions for how to solve problems of access.

3 Solutions to lack of direct access

An important aspect on which researchers into early learning agree is the need for children to combine their play and exploration between indoors and out.[21] So it seems obvious that one of the necessary elements of outdoor learning should be a designated outdoor space leading directly out from the inside. Even so, some premises where young children are registered to be cared for and educated have no direct access to an outdoor area. It seems unbelievable that settings full of active young children contrive to thwart their development by forcing them to use small, controlled movements for long periods of time. The problem has become much worse since four year olds have been propelled into reception classes in primary schools, as many of these classrooms are more fitted to older children. In some primary schools I have even been given the rationale that 'the smallest children get the smallest classroom'. On the contrary, the smallest children need the largest space.

Some practitioners are lumbered with working in places that are unsuitable for young children because they were registered as settings in the past. But imaginative practitioners have always found ways of overcoming obstacles that are thrown up by unsuitable premises – and now that the QCA's early learning goals clearly state the requirement for outdoor space(see p. 7), all practitioners must find such solutions.

Some real solutions that practitioners have found to common obstacles are given below and may be helpful to those in similar situations.

Shared premises and no direct access

Many early years settings are housed in premises where there is apparently no direct access to the outdoor space. When I first talked to one supervisor, she described her practice in such a setting and the problems it creates:

When the children arrive in the morning they are all inside until after the together snack-time (about 10.30 am). Then, if it is a nice day, we all go out and play with trikes, other wheeled toys and some bats and balls. This is our way of doing things for two reasons. First, we have to share the premises with other groups and second, there is no direct access to the outdoor area. While the children are outside the helpers can begin to clear the hall ready for the next users. We have noticed, however, that some children (especially the boys) are anxious to get to a particular trike. They race outside shoving others out of the way. Children who have been really mature and occupied all the morning become over-excited, uncooperative and aggressive and that leads to tears.

Having identified these problems, the staff began to look at what they had previously thought of as 'no direct access': the route from the hall to the garden. It consisted of a short corridor with the garden door at the end of it. There were two doors in the corridor, both of which could be shut and locked. There was one way off the corridor in another direction, to the main front door.

A scheme to stop the timetabling of garden time and allow the children to move freely between out and in was discussed at a parents' meeting. The educational and developmental reasons for the change were put to the parents who thought it a safe and good idea.

We decided to make a record of the change from all out/all in to free choice between indoors and outdoors using photographs, and jotted down some of the children's reactions. We explained to the children about the route to the garden and how they could go out to the garden when they wanted. At first the children behaved as they had before but, as it dawned on them that what had previously only been available to them for a short time was not going to be taken away from them, they settled down and began to play happily inside and out.

The supervisor and staff noticed four outcomes from their change:

1 'We became committed to making the outdoor area more interesting and stimulating to the children.'
2 'The boys chose to spend more time than previously with adults in activities like gardening and sweeping leaves.'
3 'The children had much more time in the garden.'
4 'The parents noticed positive differences in the behaviour of their children at home.'

The staff had found a way to give the children their entitlement to outdoor space safely.

The outdoor area is a car park in the evenings and everything must be cleared away

Heather and her staff in a private nursery in Newcastle-upon-Tyne are so committed to outdoor play that they set up and clear away equipment every day, winter and summer.

A temporary grant provided the means for an artist to work with the two to five year olds for two weeks in the car park. The results were stunning. Using only cardboard boxes and string, cellophane, crepe paper streamers and masking tape, the children constructed houses, boats and amazing fantasy worlds. Heather and her staff observed children discovering how to make friendships through shared intentions and revealing problem-solving abilities that were remarkable. Best of all, the children were having great fun. The staff would see an apparently empty box shaking with the laughter of the children hiding inside it, who could not contain their glee.

The staff took the constructions inside each evening and put them back as they had been the next morning.

The room for three and four year olds is upstairs

A private day nursery nurse describes a common problem:

This nursery is in a large private house with a lovely garden out the back. The babies and toddlers are downstairs and the pre-school room is upstairs for the three and four year olds. Every day for two sessions we take all the children out for about half an hour. We aim to do it every day but I must admit that sometimes we think it is too cold – probably for us and for some of the children – so we end up not going out. Actually, some of the children do complain if we don't go out.

In north London, a different nursery school faced exactly this obstacle to going out. However, the staff believed so strongly that all children are entitled to outdoor play that they had the fire escape fenced in with strong and sturdy wire netting and trained and trusted the children to come and go, up and down the fire escape by themselves.

The children who have been here for a while act as role models to new children. The flow of children is never a problem. It is self-regulating because children are given the choice as to whether they want to be inside or out for one and a half hours in the morning and the same amount in the afternoon. We obviously talk to the children about being safe and sensible. Being given the responsibility, they show it. The only time I have known children to fall is stumbling upwards, but accidents just don't happen. We've had children with muscle-tone or mobility problems and they are given help by staff and they actually bring out caring qualities in the other children who go more slowly or wait or give them a hand; it is really moving to see it.

Another nursery wondered how they could have free access for their three and four year olds who were upstairs while the toddlers and babies were downstairs. They made a radical decision. They moved the toddlers and babies upstairs. As a member of staff explained: 'We reckoned that with the better staff ratio for toddlers we could probably have the little ones outside just as often if they were upstairs.'

Yet another private nursery in London bought a wagon from Community Playthings.[22] It holds six children under three years old and can be pulled along safely by one adult. Every day they have a trip to the local park where various activities are planned for the children to investigate and where there is the space and time to run and swing and stretch muscles and minds.

The door needs to be kept open for freedom of access which makes the inside too cold in winter

Many nurseries invest in an inexpensive slow-closing device. In cold weather the door needn't be left open but the children can still operate the door without it slamming shut.

No outdoor space leading directly from the playroom or classroom

In some primary schools the headteacher expects the reception children to have a playtime in the same way as older children. These headteachers may not know this is not appropriate or that playtime generates a great deal of fear and concern in four year olds in reception classes. A group of reception teachers in Haringey suggested the following solutions:

- the outdoor area should always be available, ie there should be direct access to the outdoors from the classroom;
- reception children MUST have a separate playtime apart from the older children;
- the playground should be made attractive, with seating, trees and games areas; and
- there should be areas for role play and other play facilities, books and equipment to play with.

However, if reception children *have* to have a playtime break with the older children, the following ideas may help the reception teacher to negotiate on behalf of the young child:

- have a separate playtime for young children in their first term of reception and then gradually integrate them into the main playtime;
- pair older children with younger;
- ask parents to help out with playground duties – for the first term at least – to make more adults available;

- plan for teachers and nursery nurses to go out with the children and play games with them; and
- train playground supervisors so that they are alerted to the needs of young children.

At one primary school, the reception class is on the ground floor but has no direct access to the outdoor playground. The school's headteacher told me how they dealt with this problem:

I believed that free movement for four-year-old children was essential and I had a very good teacher and nursery nurse working in my reception class whom I didn't want to lose. Together we drew up a development plan for the reception class. The most expensive part of the plan, of course, was knocking a door through from the classroom to the playground and cordoning off a piece of the playground. After that it was plain sailing. Taking the parents and governors along with us was essential and they were informed and involved every step of the way.

4 Providing an outdoor learning environment

On the edge of a small, rather bare Tarmac nursery play area were some bushes. A group of children played in and out of them, sometimes transforming leaves into plates, and sticks into knives and forks. It got muddy in the bushes after rain, and dusty in dry weather. The adults wondered whether they should allow the children to go into the bushes because a parent had complained about one child's clothes getting very muddy. Observing this play, however, they saw how much the children were drawn to the bushes and thought about why that place was so attractive to them, why the play was so fulfilling and what learning was going on. They decided that the bushes were important to the children's learning and let them continue playing there.

The possibilities for learning in your outdoor area

Taking stock of everything that is in the outdoor area – especially the fixtures like plants, surfaces, sheds, grass and walls – enables staff to be conscious of and value the potential learning opportunities for the children. The bushes in the example enabled the children to hide, transform one thing into another, imagine, make up stories, negotiate rules and roles, share and count as they experienced living things ... the list is almost endless.

One pre-school which met on church premises took stock of their outdoor assets and listed in their audit that they had:

- an area which was rarely used by any other group;
- permission to leave out tyres and crates if neatly stacked;
- a bed they could dig for plants;
- a paved, safe pathway (about 6 metres long) from the church hall to the south facing garden running between the high wall on one side and the church wall on the other (children were able to go between indoors and out by themselves);
- a triangle of grass, 8 metres × 7 metres;
- a high, padlocked wire gate out to the pavement and busy road;
- a concrete path around the grass and wider (car width) concrete area in front of the gate;
- a slight gradient down to the gate;
- a high perimeter wire fence with a high privet hedge in front of the fence and a plastered wall on the other side;

- the brick wall of the church; and
- an arched old wooden door with gothic-style hinges and handle.

When the practitioners brainstormed an educational audit of all these assets, the area began to look very exciting. Here are some of the things they listed:

- all sorts of textures to explore – hard, ridged and bumpy brick, wood, wire fencing, strange hinges;
- a concrete path for chalking – perhaps with zebra crossings or for making drawings;
- a south-facing wall for making shadows on sunny days – shadows of bodies, hands or puppets;
- a visible road for taking surveys of vehicles – how many lorries, how many red cars, etc;
- the possibility of growing vegetables and flowers;
- earth where worms, ants and snails can be found; and
- a gradient where children will experience the extra effort of pushing things uphill and rolling down.

The way that children experience everyday things is the stuff of the early years curriculum. The sounds of traffic passing the outdoor setting, a gradient calling for more effort when pushing a wheeled toy, the space in which to run, the effects of the weather – early years practitioners can help children make sense of all these, and can use them to further children's thinking.

Learning in the park

The idea that practitioners should study the outdoor environment in terms of curriculum potential is particularly relevant when there is no direct access to an outdoor area. Daily trips out, to the local park for instance, mean that children's entitlement to movement goes hand in hand with their entitlement to a relevant and extensive curriculum.

One staff group observed all the activities the children engaged in when they went out one day and found the grass had been cut and the cuttings left. In observing the children's reactions to these cuttings, the practitioners realised that the children had presented them with an amazing range of possible lines of enquiry, in curriculum terms, and the only problem was which ones to choose to follow up. Staff observed all of the reactions shown in the table opposite.

In some settings children gather and actively investigate, in similar ways, leaves, conkers and sycamore spinners which fall onto their outdoor area in the autumn.

Children's reactions to grass cuttings: staff observations

Threw it	Gathered it	Sensed it	Imagined with it	Used it to
■ great exuberance and joy (physical, personal social and emotional); ■ chasing and tumble play (physical, personal, social and emotional); ■ negotiation of rules about throwing (language and communication, personal, social and emotional, creative and problem-solving)	■ words such as 'pyramid', 'triangle' and 'build it high' (mathematical, language and communication, creative and imaginative); ■ efficiency: 'we could do it quicker if we put it in the wheelbarrows' (mathematical, language and communication, social, problem-solving); ■ how big can we make the pile? (physical, social, problem-solving); ■ counting the wheelbarrow trips (physical, mathematical)	what it: ■ smelt like; ■ felt like; ■ tasted like; ■ looked like; and ■ whether it was hot or cold (all language and communication, personal, social and emotional)	transformed it into food, confetti and nests, with all the associated play (physical, language and communication, personal, social and emotional, creative and imaginative)	gave grass to gerbils (personal, social and emotional problem-solving)

Equipment, resources and ideas

One of the misunderstandings about the outdoor area is that it has to be developed in a complicated way, with fundraising to buy expensive climbing frames, a safety surface and so on. It is true that some outdoor areas do have quantities of expensive equipment for which staff and parents have raised funds over several years. But the success of an outdoor area, as far as children's learning is concerned, does not lie in the cost of the equipment. What matters is the capacity of what is there to be noticed by the children (and adults), to capture their imagination and curiosity so they want to look further.

If the outdoor learning environment is well organised, children will set themselves demanding tasks which challenge all their abilities, freeing staff from a mundane supervisory role and giving them the opportunity to:

- observe and assess the children's interests and abilities in order to focus adult involvement and intervention effectively; and
- play, talk and explore with small groups and individuals without being interrupted by children who have run out of ideas.

What is provided outside extends and enriches children's experiences inside and vice versa. Many opportunities will be missed if outdoor learning merely mirrors the learning that goes on inside. To make the outside work, it is important to do more than wheel out the water tray with the same equipment as indoors. Of course, in this case, some children may choose to play in the water tray outside rather than inside but it is not extending the possibilities of water play, it is merely copying what has already gone on.

If children explore how water flows through tubes and pumps inside, how much more interesting it is to see how water can be made to run through huge pipes and gutters outside, without the fear of spilling it. Outside, children can water the plants, paint on surfaces with water, splash in puddles, feel and listen to the rain, notice evaporation, play in the paddling pool, combine water with other substances such as sand and earth, and explore water on gradients.

For disabled children water play can often engage where all else has failed, especially for children with conditions such as autism.

Buying equipment for outdoors

Before considering what equipment could enhance an outdoor area, it is first essential to run an inventory of that area to see what is there already and what is missing. The checklist on the next page can be used for this purpose.

The following ideas for resources and equipment serve the purposes given in the checklist.

Small and large equipment accessible to the children
Well-arranged storage system accessible to the children
Trolleys

Many nurseries have bought one or more trolleys which they wheel outside in the morning and, if necessary, wheel in at the end of the session. In each drawer of the trolley is kept a set of small equipment such as bats, balls and bean bags, skittles, large paintbrushes and small buckets, ropes, hats, streamers, large pieces of cloth, quoits, clip boards with pencils attached, playground chalks, gardening tools, wellington boots, dressing-up clothes, notices and labels. On the

Checklist for outdoor resources

In your outdoor area do you have examples of the following?

Small and large equipment accessible to the children ☐
Well-arranged storage system accessible to the children ☐
Access to water ☐
Places to hide and be quiet ☐
Places to dig and plant ☐
Places where animals, insects and birds will be found ☐
Support for children learning through their senses
    a range of textures ☐
    a range of smells ☐
    a range of sounds and music ☐
    a range of sizes, shapes and colours ☐
    gradients ☐
Equipment for practising skills
    jumping on and over and going through ☐
    balancing ☐
    kicking, throwing and aiming for ☐
    getting into and under ☐
    pushing, pulling and riding ☐
    sliding ☐
    swinging ☐
    climbing ☐
Equipment for sand and water ☐
Equipment to trigger imaginative play ☐
Equipment for investigation ☐
Equipment to build, haul and construct with ☐
Provision for drawing and painting ☐
Provision for speaking and listening ☐
Provision for reading ☐
Provision for writing ☐
Provision for maths ☐

Anything else?

outside of each drawer there is a photograph or a drawing of the contents and a written label, for example:

4 balls

Good organisation of the resources is, in itself, an important means of access to learning. Everyone, including the children, should know where the home base is for each item of equipment. Then the children can help themselves to this equipment and feel in charge. Children and staff won't know this by magic, they need to be trained to put things back in their right place. Some children may disappear at tidy-up time, but if there is a place for everything, tidy-up time can be a sorting and matching game that will be fun and so keep the interest of more children. To the tune of 'Here we go round the mulberry bush', you can make up a tidying song to train children to put things away and where:

'I wonder where the skittles go, the skittles go, the skittles go
I wonder where the skittles go, when it's time to tidy'

'Oh they go in a trolley drawer, a trolley drawer, a trolley drawer
Oh they go in a trolley drawer, when it's time to tidy'

It is important to give yourself and the children plenty of time to tidy up and to work out what needs to be tidied up first and what can wait until later.

Sheds

Another similar idea is from a nursery setting which has a shed in which to put all its outdoor equipment. In this case there was easy access to the shed contents for the children after the wheeled toys were taken out for use. They adapted and organised the inside of the shed as a self-service area with silhouette shapes of the resources to help children put things back and look for things that were missing. They put up laminated labels above the relevant resources in the shed such as:

■ Learn to read and write
■ Learn to throw and aim
■ Learn to skip and tie knots
■ Pretend
■ Dance

In another nursery, where they can leave out some equipment, they use an old book case to store the buckets, moulds and spades for the sand so that children can help themselves.

Access to water
Ideally, children need to have a tap outside so that they can fill buckets themselves. Otherwise a rain barrel with a tap at the foot is a good substitute.

Places to hide and be quiet
Trees and bushes, large pieces of cloth, travelling rugs over an A-frame, a play house, tent or shed – in a child's imagination a piece of cloth can become a tent or a house. Deck and patio chairs can provide good places for 'a quiet read', and reading in the tent can save the book from too much wear and tear. In one nursery they have a rocking horse under a veranda. It is a place of refuge for many a child who just wants to watch the world go by from a safe vantage point.

Some outdoor areas are sectioned off by lines of tyres or even a chalk line to indicate areas where trikes may not go. This can create places where children can feel more at peace from the bustle.

Places to dig and plant
Earth contained by a rectangle of planks can form a satisfactory raised bed with equipment such as buckets, plant pots, spades, trowels, sticks and stones. Alternatively, slabs of concrete on the earth give good places for children to work without getting muddy feet. Children will find wild life in the soil while they dig.

Even the smallest area of soil can support rows of vegetables. Planting seeds gives children opportunities to compare and sort as well as to encounter large numbers. Imagine how exciting it is to sing 'one potato, two potato' if you have grown your own potatoes, or to dig up a great big enormous turnip that you have grown and nurtured yourself. In the south of England or in a sheltered area, practitioners have attempted to grow sugar cane, banana and aubergine. Eating the produce or giving it to the nursery pets gives children a highly motivating insight into food production.[23]

Designated flower beds and vegetable patches are ideal, but tubs, lorry or car tyres and large pots filled with earth are just as good for planting bulbs, plants and vegetables.

Places where animals, insects and birds will be found
Let a part of your outdoor area become 'wild'. Put off-cuts of logs on

the earth and wait for the excitement of lifting the logs and finding creatures underneath. Snails and slugs are attracted to upside-down flowerpots. Spiders and insects such as bees, ants, caterpillars and greenfly are attracted to the growing plants. A leaky water tray sunk into the ground on a slight slant with a boggy area at one end will attract frogs and toads. Birds and squirrels like bird tables. Trees and bushes support wild life too.

Support for children learning through their senses
A range of textures
The staff at one nursery began to think of the textures in their outdoor environment because one of their children had severe visual impairment. They took an inventory of the textures and were amazed at the variety of descriptive words they were using: *hard* concrete and *soft* grass, *ridged* and *grainy* wood on the shed and the tree bark, *rough* and *bumpy* brickwork and *knobbly* pebble dashing on the walls, *smooth* paintwork on the doors and *prickly* and *sharp* leaves on the holly, and *furry* leaves on the lambs ears plant.

In becoming aware of the richness of textural experience in the outdoors for one child, the staff had, in fact, raised awareness for all.

A range of smells
It is so easy to make a herb garden with the children in any area outside, either in pots or by making a small bed and planting some mint, lemon balm, sage or lavender – all of which grow like weeds and are virtually indestructible.

A range of sounds and music
Children have always used sticks as beaters to find out about sound, and many nurseries are surrounded by railings or wire fences suitable for just that purpose. Different surfaces make hollow, loud, quiet, metallic, wooden or muffled sounds, and beaters and sticks should be available for children to experiment with sounds at their own pace and in their own time. The beaters can be stored attractively in their own container or put into a trolley drawer.

One nursery put hooks on an old clothes horse and hung various noise-making things on it, changing what was hung on the hooks according to the children's interests, for example there might be tin cans, copper piping, a cymbal or some metal chime bars. The same nursery got hold of some empty cooking-oil drums and turned them into musical drums by covering the top with rubber sheeting. The drumsticks were made of cut-down broom handles with padded heads secured with strong linen tape.

Wind chimes can be bought or, better still, made by and with the children and hung on the trees.

Thoughtful planting can also bring rewards in terms of children's sensory experiences. In the autumn poppy seed cases make the most delicate shakers and the papery noise of honesty seed heads is a sound that delights children.

A range of sizes, shapes and colours
Everything surrounding children – windows, roofs, leaves, climbing frames – comes in a variety of shapes, sizes and colours.

The children at one nursery in the heart of commercial London spent one day hunting for shapes in tall and modern office blocks around their setting. They found round, square and rectangular windows and triangular pediments, and took photos of them when they were found. The photos were made into a book, to the delight of children and parents because some of the parents worked behind the shapes in the book.

Another nursery strung up some old computer disks and the children saw the kaleidoscopic rainbow colours as they twisted in the wind and caught the sunlight.

Gradients
Your outdoor area might be completely flat, but gradients can be created in many ways:

■ planks and blocks can be used to make a ramp;
■ guttering is useful to pour water down; and
■ a see-saw and slide help children experience up and down.

Gradients come in the voice, too, as children are encouraged to vocalise coming down a slide. Other gardens have slight inclines or grassy mounds down which children can roll.

Equipment for practising skills
Jumping on and over and going through
Equipment that can be used in this way might include:

■ stepping stones sunk into the grass;
■ hoops;
■ chalk circles drawn on the tarmac;
■ planks;

- beams to jump over; and
- tunnels or offcuts of huge gas pipes to go through.

Balancing

Equipment that can be used in this way might include:

- see-saw;
- beams;
- climbing frame;
- stilts; and
- a chalk line drawn on the ground, on which children can pretend they are walking a tightrope.

Kicking, throwing and aiming for

Equipment that can be used in this way might include balls, beanbags, hoops and washing-up liquid bottles filled with water aimed at a target – perhaps a hole cut in a cardboard box or a basketball hoop on the wall.

Getting into and under

Equipment that can be used in this way might include:

- travelling rugs;
- pieces of cloth;
- tunnels;
- A-frames;
- barrels; and
- hoops.

Pushing, pulling and riding

Equipment that can be used in this way might include:

- trikes with shelves on the back for another to stand on;
- trucks;
- wooden pushchairs;
- hay carts;
- wheeled toys;
- porters' trolleys; and
- toy supermarket trolleys.

Sliding

Equipment that can be used in this way might include:

- slides;
- planks; and
- triangular blocks.

Swinging

A rope attached to the middle of a climbing frame with knots all the way up gives children the opportunity to haul up their full body weight on their arms.

Two parallel, horizontal ropes about 1 metre apart, the lower one 15 centimetres off the ground strung between two posts, allow children to swing, hold on and develop strong arm muscles as they progress sideways along them.

Climbing

The climbing frame is an important piece of equipment. Children are highly motivated to climb and, in doing so, they build up the muscles in their arms and legs while strengthening their courage and confidence. A well-anchored small section of tree trunk, begged from the parks department of the local authority, can also serve for climbing if care is taken to secure it well. Trees themselves have always acted as sturdy climbing material.

Equipment for sand and water

Sand

For this, build a children's sand pit. If one is not available or costs too much, a tyre from a large tractor or other heavy goods vehicle acts as a solid wall which can be filled with sand. Other 'pits' can be made by building a square of bricks or laying four railway sleepers on the ground.

At night, or when the children are indoors, always put a tarpaulin over the sandpit to keep rain and animals out.

Equipment that children will need for sand play includes buckets and spades of different sizes, moulds, sieves, bricks, guttering, old pots, spoons, sticks (often used as cutlery or candles) and cardboard boxes. Water should be available to the children for mixing and, due to the messy nature of sand play, a dedicated storage unit should be provided for labelled sand equipment.

Water

Nature provides some of the best equipment for learning about and playing with water: rain, puddles, dew, frost, snow and ice all have marvellous learning opportunities. Human equipment comes in the form of umbrellas, wellington boots, splash suits, buckets, decorators' painting brushes, a rain barrel with a tap or outside tap so that children can help themselves to water, a paddling pool, guttering, pots and pans. As with the sand equipment, it is best to have separate storage for labelled water equipment.

Equipment to trigger imaginative play

Imaginative play outside is play on the move. It is a world of fire-engines, horses, removal vans, ambulances, police cars, milk floats, car washes, skaters, AA vans, pizza delivery bikes, petrol tankers, Batmobiles, caravans, space ships, broomsticks, aeroplanes, ships and fishing boats. All these can link with areas inside. For example, a café inside can be equally successful as a street café outside.

The appropriate place to celebrate festivals is outside and it is important to be prepared with, for example, music on tape for dancing, dressing up clothes and ideas for making carnival floats or dragons, if celebrating Chinese New Year.

Practitioners need to be ready with resources to add to the imaginative play and keep it going. Small resources can be kept in labelled trolley drawers or labelled areas of a shed. Large and small objects for imaginative play might include:

■ Dressing-up clothes such as hard hats, overalls, rubber gloves, aprons, paint brushes and buckets, plastic milk bottles, pots and pirates' hats.
■ Play equipment such as flags, tubing, ropes, 'fire-fighter equipment', a collection of 'emergency' medical equipment, shopping baskets, shopping trolleys, a picnic hamper, suitcases, rucksacks, a cooker, steering wheels, builders' hods and ambulance stretchers.
■ Planks, crates and boxes which can be turned into counters for shops or ticket offices or ramps for mending vehicles.
■ Boxes plus rope, string and masking tape can be transformed into any imaginative object by children with or without your help.
■ Wooden houses give great scope for imaginative play as well as for climbing.
■ Trees, such as weeping willows, can be turned into dens by children, but a piece of cloth over an A-frame or tied to the wire fence and anchored about a metre away can also be very effective as a house, tent, den, lair or cave.

Add and take away the resources as interests arise and subside.

Equipment for investigation

Equipment that can be used in this way might include:
■ jars with magnifying lids;
■ magnifying glasses and sheets;

- large magnets;
- equipment for investigating sound, for example metal, wooden, rubber and plastic sticks;
- pulleys with ropes attached to provide good information about forces; and
- unbreakable mirrors which reflect light and mist up when you breathe on them.

Equipment to build, haul and construct with

Several companies produce catalogues full of equipment to encourage physical, social and imaginative development.[24] However, some of the most successful 'equipment' for outdoor learning might best be described as urban scrap. This includes:

- plastic milk and bread crates;
- guttering;
- hose-pipe pieces;
- plastic gas/water pipe off-cuts;
- traffic cones;
- cardboard boxes;
- pieces of rope;
- broom handles;
- large wooden hose reels; and
- off-cuts of cloth and carpet.

Provision for drawing and painting

Drawing

Equipment needed:

- playground chalks; and
- chalk board.

Painting

Equipment needed:

- decorators' brushes of different sizes for painting with water; and
- long lengths of paper (wallpaper roll ends) to fix to a wall for BIG collaborative painting.

Provision for speaking and listening

It may be said that children need no encouragement to speak in the garden. Indeed, relaxed children are more likely to talk to each other confidently about what they are doing. However, some equipment may encourage speaking and listening by reminding children about the many purposes of communication. This could include:

- home-made mobile phones;
- microphones;
- tin can telephones; or
- drainpipe off-cuts and funnels to shout messages into.

Ticket offices, road accident 'victims', drive-through McDonalds and garage repair shops all require imaginative children to talk and listen for a purpose.

A stethoscope is interesting for children to use to hear if their heart races after running for a long time.

Provision for reading

We live in an environment which has print everywhere, and children need to see that print has a relevance in their imaginative play. Making signs is a good way to do this. Children can be involved in making advertising hoardings and other signs which can be laminated and therefore made weatherproof. For instance, a NO ENTRY sign, a McDonalds logo and car number plates can be made. A metal board for magnetic letters and notices is also useful as they allow for quick, temporary signs to be made. Some signs that children can make and then use as triggers to play:

- car wash
- park and ride
- ticket office
- shed
- trike park
- Shell petrol sold here
- today's outdoor GAME is ...
- THIS IS OUR DIGGING AREA
- YOU CAN'T CROSS THE RIVER unless you're wearing ...
- wet paint
- A&E

Over time, you can make and store a collection of laminated signs to be available when needed, but it is important to make them with the children too.

Yellow mechanics' boxes with screwdrivers and oil cans available with AA written on the side provide another opportunity for children to associate letters with sounds.

Reference books about animals, insects and birds for children to read outside need to be available in a quiet and contained place. Fictional stories can also be re-enacted in outdoor play.

Provision for writing

This might include clip boards with pencils attached by string or Velcro and playground chalks, with chalkboards attached to the wall or fence. Writing equipment will also be available associated with the imaginative outdoor play, for example police officers will be writing down the registration numbers of the trikes which speed.

Provision for maths

Some simple ideas for outdoor maths include:

- numbered spaces in which the children park their trikes which are marked with the corresponding number;
- labels on the trolley, eg 4 skittles, 10 balls, 3 skipping ropes; and
- clipboards on which children can mark down things they have counted, eg how many lorries went past the nursery in two minutes, how many bees were seen on the flowers and how many times they rode round the path on the trike.

The garden is a good place to find natural materials for collecting, sorting, weighing and making into patterns (and all of these things might then become props for imaginative play). While materials such as leaves, grass cuttings (see p. 34), pebbles, twigs, logs or bark are being used imaginatively, children are experiencing important mathematical concepts. 'I need more spice (leaves) for my soup', 'We can put the pebbles into a pattern on the ground – a circle, big ones then little ones – and we can count them, too.'

Large egg timers are used by many nurseries as a way of giving fair turns to those who want to ride on the trikes.

There are maths games from other cultures that can be taught, eg boules or oyo.

Do you really need to buy it?

Going through the checklist on page 36 and considering all the issues that spring from it (pp. 35–46) will have helped establish the areas for which you are well provided and those which might need some new resources, and even some expenditure on equipment. Once that has been established, it is important to reflect on the quality of what you intend to buy:

- Can the children use this piece of equipment in a number of ways or has it just one purpose? (For instance, do you buy a perfect replica of a real pram or a cart with a handle? Which gives more scope for the imagination? With the scaled-down pram, the imagination has nowhere to go; all the 'work' has been done for the child. The cart can be lots of things.)

■ Can this piece of equipment be played with by two or more children or only one at a time? (For example, is there an alternative wheeled toy to the trike which causes such difficulties in turn taking?)
■ Can this piece of equipment be played with by children at different stages in their development?
■ Is there a balanced range of equipment made of natural materials, metal and plastic?
■ Is this piece of equipment worth the expense – will it last?

It is also important for children to see practitioners using their imagination to make home-made resources. This gives children a good model of making play props for themselves.

5 Developing outdoor teaching skills

Participating with children in spontaneous play, talk and exploration is what should take up most of a practitioner's time outside. A sound knowledge of how children develop, their individual needs, and the experiences we need to offer children to help them think further informs our practice outdoors and affects the quality of interaction. There's a lot to have going on in our heads all at once.

Anyone learning how to drive a car has to think through every procedure in order simply to move forwards. It is such hard work that learner drivers are often exhausted after a lesson – especially after the first few. By contrast, an experienced driver can get from A to B in the car without sparing a thought for the actual process of driving, although if something unusual occurs that same driver will respond to the situation on reflex, because their understanding of driving procedures has been internalised through practice. Similarly, there are skills of interacting with young children that must be thought about and practised before a practitioner can draw on them professionally.

It is often hard for the people who are said to be 'naturally good' with children to realise that it is important to analyse and reflect on what it is that makes them tune into children so easily. It is essential to become conscious of what works and what does not, otherwise the day comes when a practitioner cannot rely on enthusiasm or 'loving being with children'; when challenging children concern and test them or when they are tired and under stress – and then they need to use all the conscious knowledge they have about their skills as an educator.

Practitioners are interested in and learn from what goes right or wrong and why a certain approach succeeds or fails. This habit of reflecting on how well we interact with children means that we develop as professional educators. Our initial training is only the beginning of the endless journey of growth – and all this is of course true whether we are working with children inside or out. So what are the specific characteristics of working with young children outside? Certainly, more care needs to be taken over maintaining a safe but challenging environment, and practitioners must learn about and be enthusiastic about the environment – that means learning to love slugs. At the heart of outdoor practice, however, is the need for practitioners to know how differently children behave outside (running, jumping, shouting, playing rough and tumble) and to observe, support and assess children's development, particularly their physical development, and its impact upon all-round progress.

It is crucial for young children to learn how to move skilfully, both for movement's sake and for the other skills that it helps develop – skills that, for instance, make it possible for children to learn to write.[25] Giving children the opportunity to use their bodies imaginatively as they move and play on stimulating equipment can help them develop mature physical skills more quickly. Practitioners play a crucial part by providing the right equipment so that children's physical play will spill into all areas of their development, not least the development of confidence. Staff also need to give children ample time to become engrossed in practising their physical skills outside, because if we trust them to be in charge of their own learning they will develop more quickly socially and emotionally as well as physically, and prove that our trust is not misplaced.

However, giving children the space to explore their physical skills is not enough in itself. We mustn't stand back, assuming that just by providing the space and the climbing frame things will proceed naturally. If physical activities are seen to have low status – in that they are activities where the teacher does not intervene and the children 'just play' – then the value of physical play to children's all-round development of children will be missed.[26]

Too often children are turned loose on various forms of equipment and expected magically to develop efficient forms of movement behaviour on their own. Only through wise guidance, thoughtful interaction and careful planning can we assure proper development of children's movement abilities.[27]

Clearly, where staff relish outdoor play, children catch their enthusiasm. Conversely, where staff do not enjoy being outside or are confused about their role outside, children get bored and vie for attention, creating a less-relaxed environment where accidents are more likely to happen. Whatever the outdoor area, be it a garden at the back of the setting, a local park or a tiny patch of green, we need to play with the children as playful educators every day.

Knowledge of children's development

Perhaps the most important piece of knowledge about children's development is to understand that each child develops in a completely individual way and at their own pace. The skill is then to respond to a child in keeping with that individual development. Most practitioners working with young three year olds know that they will come downstairs one step at a time, planting both feet safely on each step before moving on to the next. But this knowledge is only useful if practitioners combine it with an ability to recognise the right moment to hold out a supporting hand and encourage a particular child to try using alternating single feet for each step.

It is important to know broad norms of development, or developmental milestones,[28] but even more important to recognise that they have a fairly limited use because children are so different in their development. To help children become physically mature, adults need to respond to the abilities children seem to display naturally. However, when we know it is in the nature of four year olds to be argumentative with each other, to be cheeky and to answer back, then we don't feel worried or threatened and instead are pleased that they are showing expected signs of their growing confidence and independence.

As practitioners, what we really need to know are the basic movement skills. As we observe children playing outside, they are also practising these skills which are the foundation of all sports and dance. We can make them aware of their achievements in this important expressive area as they move and develop, and enrich their vocabulary at the same time. One nursery put up the following notice outside and laminated it to remind staff to observe, comment and question children about the various ways in which they move outside.

Basic movement skills

As you interact with the children, observe how they move and encourage them to move in the same and different ways, if it is appropriate

■ Children moving in different directions: forwards, backwards, sideways, up, down.

■ How children move: fast, slow, with energy, tensely, relaxed, strongly, lightly, scuttling, shuffling.

■ What children do with their bodies: turn, twist, rise, sink, advance, retreat, bend, stretch, wriggle.

■ What shape they can make with their body: round, long, wide, twisting, symmetrical, straight.

■ The names of their body parts: head, hands, fingers, wrists, elbows, arms, shoulders, bottom, legs, knees, toes.

■ How they travel: in a curve, in a zigzag line, in a straight line, along the ground, up in the air, towards, away.

■ Where they travel: around, between, under, over, through, alongside.

Identifying patterns of behaviour (schemas)

Increasingly, practitioners are finding that a knowledge of individual children's patterns of action or 'schemas' is helpful when describing their learning behaviour.[29] These schemas reveal the kind of movement and investigation that individual children are most interested in, and are particularly noticeable outside because a well-planned outdoor area offers children more opportunities to explore possibilities and to make choices.

Observing and identifying schemas allows practitioners to make sense of what some children are doing so that behaviour which, for example seems to display a child's lack of concentration, might show itself to have a clear methodology after all. Practitioners are less likely to cut across a child's line of enquiry if they understand the general purpose behind it and, instead, can offer support based on a more accurate knowledge of what is absorbing the child. For example, if a child is observed pretending to fire guns, a practitioner who understands schemas of behaviour knows that squirting water at a target may be a good replacement activity for that individual child (see p. 17 for discussion about serving boys' needs).[30]

Some children display one schema at a time and others display a cluster.

Trajectory – straight lines

This is one of the most basic and common schemas. A child who is interested in vertical trajectories, or up and down movements, might:

- jump up and down;
- like building the crates high;
- bounce balls;
- climb up and down ladders; and
- enjoy whizzing down the slide.

A child who is interested in horizontal trajectories, or side to side movements, might:

- place objects in a row;
- like to play at firing guns;
- like to squirt water at a target;
- enjoy pushing a pram or trolley;
- constantly walk on lines; or
- like sweeping the leaves, snow or puddles.

Transporting

Children fascinated by moving objects or themselves from place to place might:

- carry bags containing various objects;
- push prams or a trolley with objects or people inside them;
- carry water in a bucket from place to place;
- carry planks and bricks around outside; or
- be the bus driver and take the others to the seaside.

Enclosure
A child who is interested in enclosure might:
- build enclosures with crates etc, perhaps calling them boats, ponds or beds;
- leave the enclosure empty or carefully fill it in; or
- put an enclosing line around paintings and drawings.

Enveloping
This involves children covering or wrapping things or themselves and is often an extension of enclosure. Children interested in enveloping might:
- completely cover objects with travelling rugs;
- wear 'dress-ups' like mechanics' overalls, hats and scarves;
- wrap dolls or teddies in a blanket in the 'pram';
- wrap themselves in a blanket or be a 'worm' in the plastic tunnel; or
- fill bags with lots of leaves or small equipment.

Rotation
A child who becomes absorbed by things which turn might:
- go round and round any column or 'fire-fighter's' pole until dizzy;
- explore with taps, wheels and cogs;
- construct objects with rotating parts in wood or scrap materials; or
- love cars, trucks or anything with wheels that turn.

Connection
A child interested in joining things together might:
- use string, rope or other materials to tie objects together, often in complex ways; or
- enjoy toys that involve joining pieces together, such as a train track.

Early learning goals

As they help children develop their own skills at their own pace, practitioners also need to bear in mind what they *intend* children to learn and what children are *actually* learning. This is quite a balancing act.

The Qualifications and Curriculum Authority has published a set of goals which they expect most children to have achieved by the end of the reception year.[31] All the learning goals can be achieved in a stimulating outdoor environment although, since the outdoors is generally more suited to physical development and movement, practitioners need to be especially aware of how children are using their bodies to express themselves.

A thorough knowledge of the early learning goals enables practitioners to play around with them in the sure knowledge that if an experience is worthwhile it will be covering most of the learning goals. On pages 54–56, there is an example of how one practitioner, Gill, addressed several early learning goals through one activity, and the lines of enquiry that were linked to it.

Observation as the key to planning and assessment

To interact more effectively with children outside, it is crucial to identify what they are actually doing by observing them. It is then possible to scan mentally a wide range of interactive techniques to find the most appropriate. The right question or comment might present itself automatically, but it is important to think fully about whether that question or comment has really helped the child to think further.

When tidying up at the end of a day one practitioner was heard to say:

> I wish you'd seen what Joe did on the climbing frame this morning. He got two crates and built them up, and tried so hard to reach the horizontal bars and swing from them. It was a great struggle but he made it. Then he tried it with three crates, I suppose to see if it would be easier to reach and swing. He had to do it over and over before he succeeded because the top crate kept falling as he stood on it. He really persevered.

This practitioner was clearly very involved in what Joe was doing, and a systematic breakdown of the observation could turn the practitioner's simple enthusiasm into a clear interpretation of what Joe was learning as he climbed. This would help the setting plan for his future learning. A question-and-answer format might work in this case:

1 What movements is Joe interested in and which was he actually practising?

- *locomotor movements:* climbing, jumping and swinging;
- *stationary movements:* bending, stretching, twisting and turning;
- *gross motor movements:* gripping and letting go.

✗ Example →

Addressing several early learning goals at once

Gill is playing 'dustcarts' with a group of children. The dustcart game began spontaneously yesterday when the children were loading up carts with all the small equipment they could find lying about. Afterwards, Gill and another practitioner brainstormed which of the early learning goals this activity might cover. The next day, Gill and a group of interested children made a 'dustcart' out of a large, tough cardboard box and attached it to a trike with a rope. Because Gill used the learning goals to guide her in what she wanted the children to learn, she was prepared with questions, new words, resources and an outdoor experience (making the dustcart) that would fit in to the children's own theme. When she evaluated the children's learning from this adult-supported experience, Gill discovered that the children had had a very rich opportunity in terms of the learning goals.

In deciding what she wanted the children to learn, Gill used general questions that she always asked herself when planning an activity (italicised comments in brackets clarify the purpose behind Gill's questions).

Gill's questions
1 What is the children's current interest? *(This is the learning outcome focus.)*
2 What do I want the children to learn from this activity in terms of knowledge, skills and attitudes? *(These are the learning objectives and are related to the early learning goals.)*
3 Using play, first-hand experience, exploration and/or discussion:
   ■ what experience am I going to plan?
   ■ what words will I use?
   ■ what questions will I ask?
4 What resources will support this learning, both inside and out?
   What/who will I have to identify, find, beg, borrow, buy, gather together or learn (eg, will I learn a new song or poem, or make new story props or dress-ups or invite a visitor to come in?
5 Which children will be involved in the activity?
   ■ Which children will I focus on, and why?
   ■ Will the group be self or adult chosen?
   ■ How and where will they be grouped, inside or out?
6 Which adult will plan/lead the activity?
7 How will I know if the activity has been successful? *(Assessment against the learning objectives in point 2 above.)* Check by:
   ■ asking;
   ■ observing;
   ■ listening to hear if the children are using the new words introduced; and
   ■ seeing if the children are repeating the activity at their own pace.

8 How did it go and what will I do next from what I observed and heard from the children's reaction? *(This is the final evaluation of the activity and ideas for future development.)*

Gill's answers

This is how Gill answered the questions in relation to the dustcart project:

1 The children are interested in the dustcart game.
2 Leading from that interest, I would like the children to gain the following knowledge, skills and attitudes:
   - *personal, social and emotional* – an interested, excited, confident and motivated group of children learning to work together and listening to each other's suggestions;
   - *knowledge and understanding of the world* – (a) household rubbish is collected by refuse collectors, (b) insight into the contribution of refuse collectors to the community, (c) mapping the journey of a refuse collector, including words like 'road' and 'street';
   - *technology* – planning, designing and solving problems while making the dustcart;
   - *mathematics* – (a) mathematical vocabulary of the different two- and three-dimensional shapes needed to build the dustcart, (b) counting and estimating skills needed to work out house numbers, heavy and light rubbish and the number of journeys to each house made during a month;
   - *language* – using appropriate vocabulary and clear instructions;
   - *literacy* – (a) registration number on dustcart, (b) writing on the side of the dustcart;
   - *physical* – movement of lifting and weight and pulling empty and full boxes.
3 Using play, first-hand experience, exploration and/or discussion:
   - the experience I will plan is to make a dustcart out of boxes to sustain play the children are already enjoying;
   - I will use the following words – bin, rubbish, full, empty, heavy, light, house numbers, litter, 'one bin to one house', street, etc.
   - I will ask the following questions: What does a dustcart look like? How will we make the cart? How will we join it to the trike? What do the refuse collectors do? How could we make it move? Where will it go when we've finished it? What colour will we paint it? Will it have any writing or numbers on it? How much will it hold when it is full? Is it harder to pull when it is full of rubbish? Does the van make a noise? Can men and women be refuse collectors?
4 I need the following resources: one or two large cardboard boxes and other urban scrap, string, sellotape and rope, something (a crochet hook?) to make a

continued

hole in the box for string to go through, a poster or photo of a dustcart, large paint brushes, paint, a camera. While the children are painting the dustcart we could sing: 'Here comes the refuse collector, to your house, to your house (repeat) to your house today.'

5 Tom, Matthew, Kobir and Leon will be involved in this outdoor activity because they started the dustcart game yesterday, so making the cart will be directly extending their own interests.

6 I will plan and suggest the activity to the children.

7 The activity was successful in the following ways: The children (especially Tom and Matthew) became engrossed in the making of the cart and quickly wanted to begin to collect rubbish (leaves) and load the cart up. Leon listened to the others' suggestions and said: 'That's a good idea, Matthew!' Very good suggestions from Kobir about how to join the boxes together. Suggestions came from the children to make dustbins to collect and empty. No one suggested painting the cart today, in spite of the photo of the yellow dustcart on display. Maybe they will do so tomorrow. Good vocabulary used by all. The children liked to join in with the song.

8 Evaluation and future development: The children are very interested in transporting. Tomorrow I will observe the play and then, with some other children, pretend to be a householder asking the refuse collectors to collect, take away and transport my rubbish, as I want them now to play with the dustcart with their added knowledge.

Other ways of planning activities linked to the early learning goals are provided on pages 62–63 and pages 65–69.

2 Which early learning goals in physical development was Joe demonstrating that he had accomplished?
■ travelling around, under, over and through climbing equipment;
■ moving with confidence, imagination and in safety;
■ moving with control and coordination.

3 What should I be doing now to further Joe's thinking? There are many teaching techniques for interacting with active children on the move. Knowing which one to use and when is a skill that we get better at with practice. Here are some of the techniques that might further Joe's learning:
■ *Describing:* If the practitioner says something like, 'Now you have balanced three crates to climb on,' Joe has been given the vocabulary that is linked directly to what he is doing.

■ *Documenting:* By writing down what Joe did, drawing a sketch, taking a photograph or using a video, the moment of Joe's climbing can be captured and this will help him recall and describe his achievement days after the event.

■ *Encouraging:* A smile or saying 'you are doing really well' will raise Joe's self-esteem. Practitioners tend to overuse this type of vague interaction. It is really only helpful when children know exactly what they are doing well or what is meriting the smile.

■ *Feedback:* Saying something like 'Now you have built a tower of three crates is it easier to reach the bars?' would give Joe precise information so that he could think about what to do next.

■ *Observing:* A written observation of what Joe did provides all the practitioners in the setting evidence of his progress (see pp. 58–59).

■ *Questioning:* Some questions would help Joe reflect on his learning and challenge him to think really hard about the part he played in his own progress and how adults and other children can help him to learn. The following are general questions that could be used in most situations with most children:

– How did you do that?
– Could you do that before?
– How did you learn that?
– How can I help you?
– What do you want me to do?
– How will you learn it then?[32]

Other teaching techniques to choose from include:

■ modelling and demonstrating (doing it yourself);
■ pretending (playing alongside children);
■ suggesting another way of doing things; and
■ telling and instructing how to do things (but use this sparingly).[33]

Professional observation is the key to all successful work with young children. Observation depends on our knowledge of childhood and how children develop, and our knowledge of individual children and their families. The more we know what children are like, what they can achieve and what they are interested in the better is our chance of:

■ forming a good learning partnership with them and their families;
■ targeting our planning to individual needs and enthusiasms;
■ identifying and responding to disabled children and those with special educational needs;
■ being fair when we assess children's progress; and
■ recognising whether the learning programme we have offered is successful.

Personal observations

If this form of observation is used in a setting, practitioners are constantly on the look-out for signs of children's 'significant achievement'[34] which are mentally noted as they interact with the children. These observations are jotted down at the time, shared with the rest of the team and a parent and written up in the child's profile of achievement.

Vicky Hutchin's book gives an example of a short personal observation: 'Alan climbed to the top of the climbing frame and down again independently and confidently, without encouragement from an adult. He said: "I can do it now all by myself."'[33]

To the inexperienced, this observation might seem of little consequence, but a skilled early childhood practitioner knows about children's stages of physical development, about Alan and his family circumstances and about the rest of the staff team.

The key person added the following observation to Alan's assessment profile:

Date	Observation (note context)	Areas of curriculum	Planning support to further development
12 September	Alan climbed to the top of the climbing frame and down again independently and confidently without encouragement from an adult. And said 'I can do it now all by myself'.	■ physical development ■ attitudes to learning: confidence, perseverance	■ share observation with Alan about his achievement ■ talk to Alan's mother ■ share information with the rest of team to ensure consistency of approach ■ continue to monitor Allan's progress in climbing

The key person knew Alan was proving that he had:
- ■ the attitude and disposition to learn – motivation, energy, confidence, concentration, courage, control, perseverance and bodily awareness;
- ■ knowledge – that bodily movements can be controlled and coordinated;
- ■ understanding – of possible dangers, of his body and what it could do; and
- ■ skill – to control his body, coordinate his movements, climb and hang on, and use his growing strength.

The practitioner also knew from talking to Alan's mother that he had been protected from physical risk (for completely rational motives) and that when he first came to nursery his movements were stiff and stilted. She knew from his written profile that she and the rest of the staff team had been monitoring Alan's physical courage and risk-taking and that she could celebrate this achievement with them as well as with Alan and his mother.

Planned observations

These observations are longer and focus on particular children, specific areas of the curriculum or particular concerns. They are systematic. For example, a nursery might operate the key-person system where one member of staff is responsible for the records of eight children. That person may decide to observe each of these children for ten minutes once every month, concentrating on a specific area of development. It is important that the way in which a child uses the outdoor area is recorded.

Sample planned observation

The following observation was part of the systematic survey of all key children at the setting.

Leyla's key person has been timetabled to observe Leyla on Monday morning, between 9.30 and 10.45, when he is on the rota to be outside. In that time Leyla plays with Dejaune and is observed. The practitioner wrote down what he saw.

Leyla and Dejaune (both three years) are playing alongside the sandpit outside. It is a cold day and they have the choice of being inside if they want. They both have their coats on and the cold is the last thing on their minds because they are absorbed and concentrating on their chosen task. A toy cooker, some old pots and cooking utensils are available and a pan is on the cooker full of sand. Leyla has established her job as pouring a little water into the pan and Dejaune mixes the water into the sand in the pan. 'You mix it,' Leyla says. It requires quite a lot of effort to move the sand around the pan and Dejaune experiments with different grips on the spoon before he is satisfied with one. Leyla moves between pouring the water into the pan on the stove and into a yellow bucket full of sand about two metres away. She makes two journeys before all the water in her jug is gone. She runs off to get more water and repeats the procedure. Dejaune mixes more water into the sand in the pan.
They stay at this activity for about three-quarters of an hour.

Suggested framework for analysing planned observations

Three year olds often need play things which remind them of familiar objects to trigger them into imaginative play. Leyla and Dejaune seemed to be 'cooking a meal'. Why did they choose to be outside when they could have played the game inside? What were they learning and how were the staff supporting their development through child-friendly provision? Did it help their learning that they could mix sand and water?

Good observations keep adding to the cumulative assessments of children's progress and make the job of working with young children increasingly interesting and fulfilling. Observation is also key to planning the curriculum for groups of children and for individual interests.

Before embarking on a series of planned observations, it is useful to devise a general framework that will help to highlight the significance of each observation. The following questions provide one framework by which Leyla's key person might have analysed his observation, though different settings may have different priorities.[36]

1 What is the significance of this observation?
   - Does it reveal progress or regression in the child's development?
   - Does it reveal the development of a new interest or skill?
   - Does it reveal a change in attitude, social behaviour or feelings?
2 What does the observation tell us about the child's interests, skills, experience, attitudes, key knowledge or schema in terms of:
   - personal and social development?
   - language and literacy development?
   - mathematical development?
   - knowledge and understanding of the world?
   - creative development?
   - physical development?
3 What do we want to add to this child's record?
4 What does the observation tell us about how the provision supported this child's learning?
5 How can we plan to support and extend this child's learning?
6 What will come next? Can the child repeat this experience?
7 What do we need to provide next?

In this chapter we have looked at the importance of using a range of skills to 'teach' children outside. Teaching children effectively means selecting the next step to help children grow. The basis of good teaching is knowing our children through observation and discussion with their parents and other staff. Interacting with all our children, not just the 'easy' ones, and knowing how to intervene in their play appropriately, is a skill which we never stop developing.

6 Planning the outdoor curriculum

Planning from children's interests

Planning for the diverse needs of a group of young children is a complex task as it has to take account of each child's rate, or style, of learning and refer to the children's current observed needs. Only planning that is based on the current needs of children will give satisfaction to both children and staff.

We can always rely on a group of young children to ask us what we are doing as they cluster around willing to have a go at an adult-led activity. On the whole they do as they are asked and follow instructions because children want to please us. They survive by tuning into adults' wants and intentions and thrive on our attention. This being so, how can we be sure that the activities we plan for children are based on their interests and not our own assumptions of what they are interested in?

The education of young children is a value-laden process. Our practice reflects what we really believe and not always what we say we believe, so it is important to base planning and practice on a clear set of principles (see box on p. 64). If these are stated in policies or displayed on noticeboards, then we have a means of evaluating what we do (see Chapter 8). Some very important principles, which might be inserted into a policy, are given in the box.

Planning single activities

Before the session, write down:

- what you want the children to learn;
- which words you will use and questions you will ask;
- what reaction you expect; and
- what resources you will need to take with you (for example, if you are going to make a home-made book about your hunt for snails or slugs, make sure there is a film in the camera).

Consider which children will benefit most and how you will record and evaluate the experience. Afterwards write about what happened, whether you thought it went well and why. Store that plan as a record and reference for you and others to use another time. The evaluation will give you the information for future planned activities.

See the example planning sheet for a single planned activity on page 62–63. (For examples of longer-term plans, see the examples of

✻ Example

Planning sheet for a planned activity based on the story book *Handa's surprise*[36]

Early learning goals	Learning objectives *What do I want the children to do? Which of the early learning goals do I want to focus on?*	Activity *What experience am I going to plan so that the children will have an opportunity to learn both inside and out? What will I do? What words will I use? Which questions will I ask?*	Resources, in and out *What will I have to identify, find, beg, borrow, buy, gather together or learn?*
Personal, social and emotional development			
Language and literacy development			
Mathematical development			
Creative development, including art, music and dance			
Physical development	to practise balancing	balancing baskets on heads while walking, as in *Handa's surprise*. I will join in by walking along in a straight line using words like 'balance', 'fall' and 'dropping'.	baskets of different shapes and sizes: camera to take photos for a book about balancing; a chalked straight line and a zig-zag line to walk along
Knowledge and understanding of the world (science, technology, IT, history & geography)			

Groups *Which children will I focus on, and why? How and where will they be grouped?*	Evaluation *What did I observe the children doing that was significant? Will I add anything to a child's profile?*	Future planning *What will I plan to do next from what I observed of the children's reactions?*
	■ taking turns, especially Roddy; ■ laughing and having fun; ■ selecting the activity	
	Increased vocabulary as they retold the story in action	■ tell *Handa's surprise* at story time ■ use new words learnt while balancing ■ make a book about balancing different objects, using photos
	Children found objects to put in the basket.	Put 5–10 balls in the basket, then take one out: 'How many balls are in the basket now?'
	Roddy said to Leon: 'You pretend to be the elephant taking the mango from my basket'. Good recall of story details.	Some children might pretend to be animals. Can they match the animals to the fruit? Act out story.
self-chosen group	Sally and Rhona particularly skilled at balancing; they talked about *Handa's surprise* and wanted to put balls in the baskets to represent fruit and to make it more difficult for themselves	Repeat the activity, but add 5–10 balls to put into the baskets, and steps for the children to stand on, to remove the balls from the baskets as children pass.
	Jess asked why the basket kept falling.	Test out more efficient ways of carrying the baskets. Did Handa have a good idea? (Look in the book.) Could we make a pad like hers to help us balance?

Principles of planning for outdoor learning

- Children need space outside.
- Safety is paramount outside, but not to the exclusion of risk and independence.
- Children need the outside area available to them most of the time.
- Children need long periods of uninterrupted time to go between the outside and inside at will.
- The whole curriculum can be covered and discovered through outdoor activities.
- Children need the outdoor layout and routine of the day to be predictable.
- Planning for outside activities needs to be based on observation of individuals and groups of children indoors and outdoors (the outdoor area is often the best place to get to know about children's current interests).
- A practitioner can judge equipment and activities outside to be worthwhile when they are open-ended enough to have most of the areas of the curriculum learning in them.
- Practitioners need to enjoy being outside and be committed to developing the outdoor area.
- Practitioners need time allocated in which to share their observations with each other and with parents, and to display their plans.
- 'Garden-keeping' tasks, where adults and children work together to maintain the outdoor area are planned and educationally valued.
- Planning should be flexible enough to respond to surprises, enthusiasms and discovery.
- Planning needs to allow children outside in all weathers.
- Practitioners should know and be clear about their role as educators outside. They are not merely supervisors in the outdoor area.
- Practitioners need appropriate training to learn more about how to manage outdoor learning.
- Practitioners should never be complacent. They should request, demand and fundraise for appropriate space, access, equipment and storage areas to ensure good outdoor provision.
- We are the children's only advocates for an appropriate environment.

Gill on pages 54–56 and the Mrs Mopple topic plan on pages 66–69. These both involve multiple activities and multiple outcomes.)

A store – or bank – of previously successful activities or lists of new ideas provides resources for the future. See pages 70–75 for detailed activity banks that respond to sudden changes in the weather.

Patterns of planning

There are many ways to plan outdoor learning, and finding the way that suits your group and setting is one of the first tasks. Here are some of the patterns of planning that practitioners use:

- topic planning (below);
- planning for 'spontaneous' events (see pages 69–76);
- planning for games and songs (see pages 76–80); and
- planning from and for individual children from skilled observation (see Chapter 5).

Topic planning

Many settings find that planning around a single theme is useful. Themes, or centres of interest, can be focused on a particular aspect of the curriculum, such as sound and music-making or mini-beasts and living things in the garden. In the late autumn, some settings may choose to focus on light and darkness because there are festivals of light (Diwali) and Bonfire Night with local fireworks displays and bonfire events which children will have experienced. Light and dark also lead into Hanukah and Christmas.

Some story books inspire children's imagination, and practitioners can explore a range of indoor and outdoor play experiences around the themes in the story book. Outside is an ideal place to re-enact favourite stories.

Whatever topic is chosen by children and adults, it is important to make it broad enough to embrace many lines of enquiry. If a group of children shows an interest in their comparative heights, a theme such as 'Growing' will include the possibility of going into the garden to measure progress of seedlings planted the previous week or discovering more about one of the children's new baby brother.

I have argued that free movement is crucial for the successful development of young children (see Chapter 1). It follows, therefore, that outdoor activities need to be integral to all planning; they are not merely add-ons. Some practitioners plan outdoor activities separately in order to focus specifically on the outdoor environment. Others see the whole learning environment inside and out as one enlarged learning area, and this is a very positive view. Of course a few activities are more appropriately carried out inside but most are suitable for outside.

The advantages of topic planning are that:

- children, practitioners and parents can unite around one idea;

- (if it is broad enough) a topic can integrate children's varying concerns and interests;
- visits and visitors can be planned in advance to maintain or initiate enthusiasm and more information; and
- a successful topic enables children to understand the satisfaction in studying deeply over many weeks.

However, topic planning will not work effectively if:

- the topic is chosen by practitioners without reference to the current interests of the children;
- the topic has no link with the outdoors and is planned for indoor activities only;
- once planned, practitioners are reluctant to abandon their plans and follow children's reactions; and
- the topic is narrow in scope and has to be changed too quickly.

In the overall plan for any topic, outdoor activities should be integrated with indoor activities. Children and practitioners are able to see that some activities are more suited to indoors or out and make their activity choices accordingly. For example, in one setting that was focusing on hospitals and health, children and adults set up a hospital area inside, but had the accident and emergency department outside. This meant that the wheeled toys could be used as ambulances, planks became stretchers and lemonade bottles were oxygen cylinders. Notices were made for reception areas where children could check in their friends who had met with 'accidents'.

Sample topic plan

The following topic plan is based on *Mrs Mopple's washing line*[38] and integrates indoor and outdoor activities.

Recognising the children's delight in the story of *Mrs Mopple's washing line*, one nursery teacher and nursery nurse planned to support and extend the group's interest in the story. When planning for this topic, they asked themselves the following questions:

- Which early learning goals can be achieved most successfully from this story?
- What first-hand experiences and imaginative play activities (indoors and out) are we providing already and how can we plan to support that learning?
- Which resources will we have to buy, collect, beg and borrow?
- Which new songs, poems and stories will we need to learn or find?
- Will there be any visits or visitors associated with the story which we need to plan for in advance?

- How can we involve the children in the planning?
- How can we challenge the stereotypes in this story?

These issues were addressed through the learning goal grid that appears on pages 62–63. (For the purposes of simplicity we have not answered all these questions directly, for example whether the nursery would have to buy or borrow resources, as for any setting the answers would follow from the resources identified as necessary.)

Early learning goals and Mrs Mopple's washing line

Personal, social and emotional

Learning goals and learning opportunities	Activities to support learning
Children continue to be interested, excited and motivated to learn Children are confident to try new activities, initiate ideas and speak in a familiar group, work as part of a group and share Children can maintain concentration	These learning dispositions of children will be identified as children take part in activities associated with this theme.
Children understand that different people have different views and that everybody should be treated with respect	■ Dressing and undressing the dolls for washing. ■ Having a discussion about whether it is fair that Mrs Mopple does all the work around the farm.

Physical

Learning goals and learning opportunities	Activities to support learning
Children move confidently and imaginatively, and in safety	Dancing with large pieces of cloth.
Control and coordination of large movements	Running in the wind with streamers or shopping bags tied to sticks.
Recognise the importance of washing and keeping clean	Washing and hanging out dolls' clothes.
Recognise that, when active, the heart rate and breathing increase, and you sweat	Tissue paper sticks to your face when you are hot from running. Why?
Small movements – cutting and joining	Use small muscles when cutting and making the washing machine out of a large box.

Language and literacy

Learning goals and learning opportunities	Activities to support learning
Children make up their own stories	Wash tub, washboard and the actual clothes props to be washed inside and out.
Children listen and respond to stories and nursery rhymes	Children listen to and play with the prepared story props associated with Mrs Mopple's theme, eg 'The sun and the wind' (an Aesop's Fable).
Children listen and respond to poems	'The wind', by Richard Edwards; 'Washing-up day', by John Agard; 'Machines', by June Mitchell.
Recognise familiar words	Making washing machines out of boxes can lead to a laundrette or dry cleaners being set up inside or outside, with the relevant words, prices and instructions laminated and left outside for play, eg 'Washing powder'; '10p a wash'; 'press the button to start'.
	■ Opportunities for book making, eg a book of instructions when the washing machines are made.
	■ Visit to a laundrette can be photographed and a book made about the excursion.

Creative development

Learning goals and learning opportunities	Activities to support learning
Explore and respond to sound, express ideas through sound and music and communicate their feelings	■ Make instruments like a guiro from plastic containers or make a huge sound collage out of boxes including the use of corrugated paper to scrape.
	■ Wind instruments: (1) music table display of pictures of instruments that you blow; (2) make trumpets out of paper and straws and blow them outside (noise doesn't matter); (3) invite a musician who plays a wind instrument or older children who play recorders, follow them round the garden in a procession; (4) make wind chimes inside out of bottle tops and string and hang them outside.
	■ Explore rhythm – learn 'Rub-a-dub-dub, three men in a tub', accompanied on the railings or other suitable surface.
	■ Learn songs to do with the story, eg 'The witch of weather', 'Blow the house down', 'Mrs Mopple had a farm' – using song props and action games.
	■ Use instruments to make machine noises like the washing machine and, moving like big machines, retell the story with instruments for the characters and the wind.
	■ Explore pitch, eg of the wind 'oooooo'; sounds that are high and low; noisy games outside.
	■ Use commercial and home-made instruments to find out about things you can scrape outside, eg railings.

Mathematics

Learning goals and learning opportunities	Activities to support learning
Sequencing	Washing the dolls' clothes, hanging them out to dry.
One-to-one correspondence	Dolls' clothes put on the right doll after cleaning. Are they on the big, middle or small doll?
Matching	Dressing up games where children match the story clothes to the animals who wore them.
Counting in pairs	Sorting washing in pairs from a store of large and small socks and gloves.
Counting and multiplication of number	Hanging the washing on the washing line with pegs – two to each garment. How many garments? How many pegs?
Exploration of 'odd' mathematical language	'Twice round the haystack' Once, twice, thrice.

Knowledge and understanding of the world

Learning goals and learning opportunities	Activities to support learning
Science – why things happen and how things work	Clothes are cleaned by washing – washing activities and experiments to see what substance washes best.
History – past and present events in their own lives	Mrs Mopple used a tub and a washboard. What do some of us use today instead? (Links with technology, below.)
Geography – features of events in nature	The weather is a geographical feature which can be explored, eg running in the wind with streamers or shopping bags tied to sticks.
Geography – features of locality	Take pictures of the trees etc, when it is windy and when there is no wind, and make a 'windy book'.
Technology – Children use technology where appropriate to support their learning: designing, cutting, joining, folding	■ Visit the local laundrette and operate the machines. ■ Visit a child's house to operate a domestic washing machine or dish washer. ■ Make a 'washing machine' for the home corner out of junk material.

Planning for 'spontaneous' events

Opportunities for capitalising on the children's enthusiasm can be missed because planning for what might and most probably will occur has not been done in advance. Many of the children will be excited by rain, wind or snow. They will want to experience it at first hand. What

Books dramatised outside

Books provide an excellent starting point for planning extensions to the curriculum. Here is an example of how a setting followed up a reading of Eileen Browne's *Handa's surprise*.[39]

After hearing the story Handa's surprise, *lots of baskets were made available outside which children could fill with things and then balance them on their heads. One practitioner supported the children's experimentation by playing with them (she wasn't very good at it and her basket kept falling off her head). Some children were skilled and others tried to find more stable ways to fix the basket and steady it. This experimentation was extended by the practitioner the next day. She suggested that they could re-enact the story with one child playing Handa and balancing the basket on her head. She could pass by the climbing frame and the children perched on it could reach out and each take one thing from the basket.* Children recalled the story and suggested more elaboration.

(For a detailed plan linked to *Handa's surprise*, see pp. 62–63)

children need is to be outside experiencing the actual feel, touch, sight and taste of the snow itself.

Can you imagine the scene of children sticking cotton wool on a paper snowman inside as the snow is falling outside? Or worse, practitioners sticking to the plans they made for the day and ignoring the chance to go out because 'it's too cold'.

Take, for example, a windy day. At some point there will definitely be a windy (or rainy or frosty or even snowy) day when the children are at the setting. But, if you are to go with the flow of children's enthusiasm, it is too late to start planning on the morning of the day. Begin to collect photographs and posters that will tie up with what might happen in the outdoor area, eg kites flying or trees blowing in the wind. Having a photograph of what happens to trees in the wind helps focus and further children's enthusiasm. It is part of long-term planning that these photos and other resources should be available, well organised and accessible. A concertina box file is ideal as it is compact. Photos can be laminated and stored in alphabetical order.

Weather boxes

Weather boxes are like banks where plans have been deposited earlier, ready to be withdrawn when needed. They might contain:

■ observations of what the children do and what they notice on a day with a particular kind of weather – perhaps a rainy day;

Windy day resources and ideas

Some children find it difficult to understand things they cannot see but air is felt as wind and children can see and feel its effect.

Observe what the children do and what they notice

■ Children run and are excited.
■ They notice:
  - the power and strength of the wind;
  - their hair blowing;
  - trees, bushes and flowers bending;
  - leaves and paper blowing about in gusts of wind.

Prepared activities to support children's enthusiasm and observations

1 Give children long strips of crepe paper, chiffon scarves and noisy cellophane as streamers. This gives their excited exuberance a purpose and focuses the children's attention on the wind (moving air). When the paper breaks, the bits can be incorporated into a 'windy day' collage or stuck on to individual paintings inside, as some children will want to represent and record their experience in the wind.

2 Very light chiffon or silk fabric moulds around and sticks to the body when a child holding it faces the wind. This experience confirms the strength of the wind and provokes movements which are the raw material of dance.

3 Make kites indoors at the junk modelling area with string and light and heavy materials, then fly them outside. Ask the children why some fly and others do not.

4 Make wind socks by sticking plastic shopping bags on sticks. The children can then feel the power of wind resistance as they run with them against the wind.

5 Any kind of washing – dolls' clothes, plastic toys, furniture, cars – can be seen to dry more quickly in the wind (evaporation).

6 Build 'yachts' with milk crates and sticks, poles and sheets or smaller ones with card or paper.

7 Display photographs of what the wind can do with captions such as 'Look how strong the wind can be!' As parents look at the photos, encourage them to reminisce with their children about their experiences of very windy days.

Bearing the list above in mind, choose which of the learning goals you will particularly focus on in the activity:

■ personal, social and emotional;
■ physical;
■ creative and expressive, and imaginative;
■ communication, language, and literacy;
■ knowledge and understanding of the world, (problem-solving, investigation of the weather, geographical, technological, scientific); and/or
■ mathematical.

continued

Resources needed
- Photographs (cut from magazines and laminated) of what the powerful wind can do to trees, houses, boats on the sea, harbour walls and people, etc.
- Coloured crepe paper for streamers.
- Sticks and plastic shopping bags for wind socks.
- Unbreakable mirrors to look at reflections of hair blowing (supplier of technology materials such as unbreakable mirrors: South London Science & Technology Centre, Wilson Road, London SE5 8PD, tel 020 7708 1372).
- Old umbrellas which will turn inside out (as in the story *The wind blew*).
- Children's plastic windmills.
- Tape recorder to record the sounds of the wind.
- Prepared sheets for the 'yacht' (sew a seam for the pole to be threaded through to make the sail).
- A camera to record experiences and for book making.
- Craft equipment to make kites using various materials.

Books and stories
The wind blew by Pat Hutchins (Red Fox, 1994)
Mrs Mopple's washing line by A. Hewitt (Red Fox, 1994)
Percy the park keeper by Nick Butterworth (HarperCollins, 1993)
We're going on a bear hunt by Michael Rosen and Helen Oxenbury (Walker Books, 1992)
'The sun and the wind', *Aesop's fables* (Puffin, 1995)
A book about kites and kite-making

Songs
A list of songs could include:
- 'Rock-a-bye baby'
  Rock-a-bye baby on the tree top
  When the wind blows the cradle will rock
  When the bough breaks, the cradle will fall
  Down will come baby, cradle and all.
- 'Let's go fly a kite', from the film *Mary Poppins.*
- 'Windy Miller's song' from the 1960s and 1970s children's programme *Camberwick Green.*

- prepared activities to support children's enthusiasm and observations on that same kind of day;
- prepared plans showing the learning goals that the practitioner focused on during previous similar days (the measure of a worthwhile experience is that it contains all or most of the learning goals; this means that you will see children covering all the goals);
- resources needed;
- books and stories relevant to weather; and
- songs and poems about weather.

Rainy day resources and ideas

Observe what the children do and what they notice

■ Children run, jump, hold out their hands and are excited.

■ They splash in the puddles.

■ They might open their mouths to drink the rain as it falls.

■ They notice:
- reflections;
- changes in the colour of the ground (wet things seem darker or shinier);
- that some things get wet but not everything absorbs water;
- that the puddles dry up when it stops raining;
- that the wet soles and tyres make prints;
- the different smell after rain;
- the rivulets of water running down the window; and
- the gurgles in the drains.

Prepared activities to support children's enthusiasm and observations

1 Make prints with the tyres of wheeled toys and wellingtons as they go through the puddles. Adults put down paper alongside the puddle so that children can see the prints.

2 Draw round the puddle with chalk or mark it with string in the morning and see if there has been any evaporation by lunchtime.

3 Re-enact *The rain puddle* story with some of the toy animals or with the children themselves. This will make the idea of reflections more meaningful.

4 Put a drop of oil or petrol on the puddle and follow up with some discussion on colours and rainbows with the children who are interested.

5 Children do some marbling – see the patterns on paper placed on top of the oily puddle then removed.

6 With the children, cover umbrellas with different materials, eg tin foil, which is exciting for sound exploration.

7 With the children, make waterproof shelters for the dolls out of 'junk' materials, eg rubbing boxes with a wax crayon, spreading PVA glue on them or covering them in plastic bags. Investigate what happens to these boxes in the rain. Working with absorbent and non-absorbent materials can begin some discussion on what is 'waterproof'.

8 Compare a doll put out in the rain in a raincoat and one in a woollen dress. Test the best ways to get the wet clothes dry.

9 After the rain, sweep the puddles and wipe seats. Often adults do these tasks but children are natural helpers if they feel they are doing a real job which contributes to the wellbeing of the community. It is also important (and simple) to justify these jobs in your written plans in terms of which learning goals they support.

10 Collect rain; make it flow down gutters and piping.

11 Measure the amount of rain that has fallen.

12 Look for snails, slugs and worms which come out in the rain.
13 Use words associated with water, such as flow, splash, dribble, drip, droplet and gurgle.
14 Put up a laminated weather chart outside with Velcro-backed pictorial symbols (sun, rain, cloud, etc.) which the children can change.
15 Set up a display in the book corner with toys placed around a mirror (as in *The rain puddle)* to link with what has been happening outside.
16 Make reflection pictures by painting a picture on one half of the paper and folding the other half onto it before it is dry.

Bearing the list above in mind, choose which of the learning goals you will particularly focus on in the activity (see the list in the 'windy day' box, p. 71).

Resources needed

■ A store of spare wellington boots for splashing sessions with a few children. Not all children will want to go out so only a few need be out at a time.
■ A store of splash suits for access to the outside even in pouring rain (supplier of splash suits: 'Muddy Puddles', Hingston Farm, Bigbury, Kingsbridge, Devon TQ7 4BE, tel 01548 810477).
■ Umbrellas, some with waterproof material removed and filled in with tin foil, absorbent and non-absorbent materials.
■ A selection of absorbent and non-porous materials, eg sponge and tin

foil.
■ Suitable dolls' clothes for wet weather for imaginative play and investigation into absorbency.
■ Brushes and cloths.
■ Guttering, tubing, funnels and piping.
■ Very small quantity of oil or petrol to put in a puddle.
■ Mirror and fabric for the book corner display (supplier: see 'windy day' box, p. 72).
■ Chalk.
■ Magnifying sheets (send for the Kleeneze catalogue: 0870 333 6688).

Books and stories

■ *The rain puddle* by Adelaide Holl (out of print, but stocked in most libraries)
■ *Mr Grumpy's outing* by John Burningham (Puffin, 1978)
■ *Noah's ark and other stories* by Selina Hastings (Dorling Kindersley, 1996)
■ *The rainbow fish* by Marcus Pfister (North-South Books, 1992)
■ *Mrs Wishy-washy* by Joy Cowley and Elizabeth Fuller (Shortland)

Songs and poems

A list of songs and poems could include:
■ 'Rain on the green grass'
  Rain on the green grass, rain on the tree
  Rain on the house top, but not on ME
■ *Rain, rain go away – come again another day*

continued

■ 'Dr Foster'
 Dr Foster went to Gloucester in a
  shower of rain
 He stepped in a puddle, right up to
  his middle, and never went there
  again!

■ 'Raining, pouring'
 It's raining,
 It's pouring,
 The old man is snoring;
 Fell out of bed
 And bumped his head
 And couldn't get up in the morning.

■ 'Incy wincy spider'
 Incy wincy spider, climbed up the
  water spout,
 Down came the rain and washed
  poor spider out,
 Out came the sun and dried up all
  the rain.
 Incy wincy spider climbed up the
  spout again.
 Make up poems with the splashing
 children as or after they splash, eg
 'Splashing in the puddles', to the tune
 of 'In and out the windows ... as we
 have done before'.

When these plans and resources are easily available, an opportunity to exploit first-hand experience of weather is not lost. Specific plans already prepared for the day can be postponed and used some other day. The important thing is that the opportunity to exploit children's spontaneous enthusiasm about natural phenomena is not wasted.

On pages 71–75 are examples of what might be included in 'windy day' and 'rainy day' weather boxes. A similar format can be used with different resources, songs and poems for snowy, sunny and frosty days which you could construct from your own observations, experiences and resources.

Ideas to support interest in flora and fauna

Children in a well-planned outdoor environment will find interesting animals and plants and bring them to your attention with joy (or disgust). The early years practitioner can always be prepared for these times of exploration in advance by preparing the plans for suitable extension activities and looking out songs, stories and poems about animals and insects. Here are just a few ideas:

■ worms – put out the collapsible tunnel so that children can 'be' worms;

■ snails – boxes are good as shell houses to put on your back and pretend to be a snail;

■ spiders – go on a cobweb hunt;

Project bee

'We have often used bees as part of a summer project. Our garden attracts butterflies and bees and we are continually seeking ways to increase their variety. Bees often give children longer opportunities for observation than faster-moving butterflies. They also use flowers in a specific way, demonstrating pollen collection visibly and providing teaching opportunities on the life cycle of plants.

We were fortunate enough to have a visitor to the school who had her own hives and she introduced the subject of pollination to the children through role play and demonstrated bee behaviour. She also brought items that gave the children some understanding of bee-keeping. Prior to her visit, we set the children the problem of developing their own honey machines. We identified specific things that a bee needs, such as a means of propulsion, a way of collecting pollen and storage facilities. We included in our long-term project music, modelling and observational painting of the flowers that the bees appeared to like. Finally, we invited our parents to a honey tea in our garden, providing them with honey sandwiches, cakes and potato salad, all made by the children.

During our extensive garden survey, we counted bees visiting one area of the garden. We made the count twice a day, the children making their own tallies on clipboards. The children noticed that there were different types of bees and that one area of difference was that bumble bees have different coloured rear ends. They were made aware that on some days more bees appeared than on others and that some bees preferred different types of plant.'[40]

- ants – examine them with magnifying sheets;
- woodlice – lift up stones and watch them move;
- birds – make hanging cakes for them out of fat and seeds;
- butterflies – give children multicoloured pieces of material for dancing with wings and plant buddleias and other butterfly-loving plants for children to watch; and
- bees (see box above).

Songs and games to play outside

One of the joyous ways to help children feel as if they belong is playing, singing and chanting games. They are most successful outside because there is space and the children can join in and leave when they want.

It is a good idea for staff to brainstorm all the outdoor songs and games they want the children to learn, then print them up, laminate the paper and display the list outside. It is so easy to forget the full range of songs and games you know and revert to only two or three favourites every time. The list should be reviewed from time to time, to make sure all the staff know the songs.

Games and songs outside should be written out as planned activities, with learning intentions, because not to do so is to undervalue their importance in learning. Most of the games and songs outside develop and refine motor skills. They also teach and reinforce many mathematical, language and storying concepts, introduce geographical words like 'near' and 'far', 'up' and 'down', 'along', 'beside' and 'through'. They help develop social interaction, speaking, shouting and listening skills and concepts of morality.

Start all group games with the children standing or sitting in a ring. To do this, get a long piece of rope, join the ends, ask the children to hold on to the rope and pull it outwards, then sit down. Make sure there are not too many children playing games at one time as it is very boring to have to wait a long time for your turn. A group should be no bigger than double the age of the child (so a group of eight is ample for four year olds). More may want to join in but if the outdoor area is interesting only a few will want to do the game.

Games to play

Dinosaur legs
(To the tune of 'Peter hammers with one hammer'.)

Start with one child who will be 'a dinosaur with two legs'. This child skips round the outdoor area singing:

I'm a dinosaur with two legs,
With two legs, with two legs.
I'm a dinosaur with two legs,
And I'm looking for two legs more.

At the end of the song, a second child joins in, and the dinosaur grows by two legs ('I'm a dinosaur with four legs ...'), then a third ('I'm a dinosaur with six legs ...') and so on.

The dinosaur could turn into a train ('I'm a great big train with one coach ... and I'm looking for one coach more'), and this is particularly useful for younger children as it involves counting in single numbers.

Hungry dragon
(To the tune of 'Jelly on a plate'.) The hungry dragon eats from the outdoor area near the setting because the children themselves are the dragon's food. Each child who is going to play, is 'planted' in the

Sample laminated list to display outside

Some songs and games

The bear went over the mountain
The big ship sails through the alley-alley-O!
The crocodile swam in the river
The farmer's in his/her dell
I went to school one morning and I walked like this
In and out the dusty bluebells
Isn't it funny how a bear likes honey?

Ring-a-ring-o-roses
Round and round the village
Row, row, row your boat (sitting in crates)
Simple Simon
Ten green bottles
There was a princess long ago
There were ten in the bed
What's the time Mr or Mrs Wolf?

'garden'. They choose for themselves what kind of food they are going to be. For instance, a child wearing an orange sweater might be a carrot, another wearing green trousers might be a bean. Or the children may pick something out of the air completely at random. A practitioner takes the part of the dragon and walks around the 'garden' singing:

When the dragon's hungry,
She's in a hungry mood,
She goes into the garden,
To look for dragon food.
(speaks) And she finds ...

[At this point, the 'dragon' stops in front of a child and asks what food they are. The child calls it out.]

(speaks) Oh I love [eg] *round red tomatoes!*

The child crawls through the dragon's legs while the adult pretends to chew and swallow. The child then holds onto the adult's waist and the growing dragon continues eating until the 'garden' is harvested.

Sharks and islands

This game requires 'islands' that have been drawn using chalk on a hard outdoor surface (or the 'islands' can be made out of hoops or tyres). The children are fish 'swimming' around the islands while an adult or child plays the shark. Suddenly, the shark calls out: 'Sharks are coming'. At that moment, all the children run for an island, as they have to be on an island (ie inside the chalk mark or the hoop/tyre) not to be caught by the shark. Children caught by the shark become sharks themselves and the game continues until all the fish have been turned into sharks.

There are lots of variations with this game. The fish might have to hop, jump, skip or walk on tiptoe around the islands – including when the sharks are coming.

Hide and seek
Teach the children how to play this traditional game using whatever facilities there are in the playground. How inventive can you be?

What's the time Mr (or Mrs) Wolf?
In this traditional game, one child (the wolf) hides their eyes while the children call out 'What's the time Mr Wolf?', creep towards the wolf and trying to surprise him. At each call, the wolf gives a time – one o'clock, four thirty, etc – and turns around to see if anyone is moving. Anyone seen moving is out. The game keeps going until the wolf suddenly calls out that it is 'supper time' and tries to catch someone. It is very scary, and lots of squealing is guaranteed.

Hopscotch
Use the traditional markings and show the children how to play. Adapt the game for little ones who can't yet hop or jump with their feet together.

Mrs (or Mr) Bear's honeypot
This game is better done sitting than standing. A child plays Mrs Bear who is 'put to sleep' in the centre of a circle of children. The 'honeypot' (which might be a beanbag or something similar) is placed behind the bear and the children chant:
   Isn't it funny how a bear likes honey,
   Buzz, buzz, buzz, I wonder why she does?
   Go to sleep Mrs Bear'
Repeat the rhyme several times, each time getting quieter while a second child – the thief – creeps up and steals the 'pot', all the while trying to do so by making as little noise as possible. The thief returns to their place in circle and hides the pot behind them. Suddenly, all the children in the circle shout: 'Wake up Mrs Bear, your honey's not there.' The bear has been listening hard while 'asleep' to try and hear where the thief came from and went back to, because now the bear has to find the honeypot. When the pot is found, the 'thief' becomes Mrs Bear in the middle of the circle.

If keys or instruments are used, they can be shaken to help the 'bear' find them.

You can't cross the river
Draw a chalk river. A child stands on one side and calls the other children across by saying, for example, 'You can't cross the river unless you're wearing ... blue.' The children who can comply (in this case, who are wearing blue) then walk, jump, hop or run across to the other side.

For younger children, simply getting across is enough. Modify for older children so that they have to get across the river without getting caught by the children who are already on the other side.

Measuring and size
Here are some variations on a simple idea to play at the end of the session if all the children are out at once:
- How long can we make a line of children stretch?
- Can we make it shorter?
- Can it coil like a snake?
- Can we snake around the play area?
- Let's make two lines (one with all the girls and one with all the boys). Which line is longer?
- Sort the line by colour of coat.
- Sort the line by size.
- Sort the line by longest to shortest shadows.
- Move around in the line. Where has the shadow gone?

Variations on running
- Can you run fast?
- Can you run slowly?
- Can you run quietly?
- Can you run noisily?
- Stop when I blow the whistle, change direction. (Take care that younger children do not run into each other when they change directions.)
- Run in and out of markers.

Rope games
Teach the children to skip over a rope that is being held by two adults.

Use two ropes of equal length and place them side by side on the ground. The ropes form the banks of a 'river'. Encourage the children to jump over this river with both feet together. Widen the river and discuss other ways to jump efficiently (eg, running and then jumping).

7 Routines, rotas and roles

In some settings the amount of time given to outdoor play is never more than half an hour, and children are often all out or all in, even when there are two practitioners to the group. Some children are therefore out when they want to be in and vice versa. When I ask practitioners why this is so they sometimes point to their curriculum plans, as if the plans themselves are driving their work with the children. But existing management structures can always be changed to make outdoor access possible; routines, rotas and roles can be reviewed.

Staff rotas

Without doubt, it is easier to *say* that timetables and rotas can be changed than to actually *do* it. Daily and weekly routines are established over a long time and it always feels safer to keep things as

---

Changing old ways

'Our nursery has 20 three and four year olds. When I started there the children went out to play for 20 minutes before lunch. Two members of staff went out with all the children and the other member of staff set up for lunch. It is a very pleasant area – French windows leading to a small garden with paths, flower beds and grass. On sunny days in summer we used to take all the nursery equipment out and were there virtually all day.

We decided to change this after we went, with our manager, on a course and heard about the advantages to the children of free access to outdoor learning. It was important that our manager went with us because she became enthusiastic too. We have started to develop our outdoor area. The children now can choose to go out as soon as they have had their breakfast or straight away if they arrive later.

One member of staff (A) goes out with the children and knows what her specific role is going to be. After three quarters of an hour another member of staff (B) joins her and does an activity with a small group of children – usually selected because they have an interest in or need for the activity. For example, yesterday it was practising catching and throwing the balls. Depending on how many children are out, A stays out and gets involved with the children or goes back inside. When A goes back inside, another member of staff (C) can do an adult-initiated activity with a group inside. It's all about flexibility really and knowing the children well.'

they are than to challenge them. But if young children are being denied access to key aspects of their development and experience, it is vital for practitioners to conquer their fear of the unknown and take an organisational step towards letting the children explore the outdoors more freely. However, free choice for whether the children are out or in does not imply free choice for practitioners.

In some settings one practitioner is responsible for the outside area for one week giving them an opportunity to sustain children's ideas over a longer period. In other settings, or at different times of the year, the rota might change every 30 minutes.

The outside area works well when practitioners, whether just two or many more, have discussed and come to decisions about:

■ their shared understanding about what the outside area is for;
■ when and for how long will they be outside; and
■ what their role is when they go outside.

Staff roles

Practitioners often feel confused about their role when they are outside, finding it difficult to decide whether they should be police constable, referee, observer, safety officer, assessor, arbitrator or instructor. To a certain extent the answer is that, out of doors, practitioners fulfil all of these roles and the skill is to respond to the children using whichever 'persona' is appropriate to each individual child and each individual situation.

However, it is possible to assign different members of staff different main roles while out of doors – perhaps on a rota basis. Knowing their primary purpose while outside means that practitioners can feel a sense of satisfaction in outdoor assignments and can feed back observations, achievements or disappointments to the rest of the staff team. On your planning sheet each day there must be a note of each practitioner's role and a short evaluation from which you can plan ahead.

The following list details the roles for practitioners with the children while they are out of doors. The list is not exhaustive, and practitioners could combine any of these roles to suit the organisational needs of any setting.

Set up equipment and evaluate its use during the session

The setting up of equipment becomes much more interesting and meaningful if a practitioner can then evaluate its purpose. To see and observe how resources are used by the children, and who uses them, means that the practitioner knows what to add or withdraw in future sessions, and what has got broken or could be unsafe. Some larger settings photocopy blank plans of the outdoor area and draw onto the basic plan where the variations to the weekly layouts will be.

Put equipment away

This is an essential 'garden-keeping' job which is made much more significant if the equipment is well organised, with small equipment in marked and labelled trolley drawers and large equipment in well-organised storage sheds (see Chapter 4). When children can help with tidying up, and everyone sees it as part of their contribution to the community, then it is not a chore but a valuable learning activity.

This job includes a timetabled maintenance check (eg the first Friday of every month) in which any equipment that is unsafe would be discarded or identified for repair. It is efficient to have a checklist of the equipment and the date when it was last checked.

Observe key child, 'focus' children or learning area

A timetable of systematic observations can be drawn up, depending on how many children one practitioner is responsible for. In one nursery each practitioner was responsible for the profiles of 15 children, and a focused observation was made of each child once every five weeks. (This worked out at three observations for each practitioner to analyse every week.) The child's progress is assessed and new targets set. Practitioners continually jot down interesting observations of children's achievements throughout the day and add these to each child's file – and for this to work, a systematic procedure must be in place or some children could slip through the net. If there is free access to the outdoor area, a greater or lesser percentage of the observations will be made in the outdoor area for the children depending on how much they use the area. (See pp. 53–60 for guidance on observation and assessment.)

Play imaginatively and partner children's spontaneous play, talk and exploration

The quality of children's learning, the length of time they spend in exploration and the imagination within their play all increase if practitioners get involved, without dominating, and show that they are interested in what the children are playing and exploring. Children are dealing with big issues in their play: life and death, illness and health, power and powerlessness, fear, courage, triumph and disaster. Outside, they are and should be very physical in their imaginative play, and it is hardly surprising that we are sometimes at a loss to know how we can have any part to play in the apparently chaotic games of superheroes. Becoming aware of the worthwhile themes to show interest in and how to participate is a professional skill that we need to keep practising. The strategies we can employ to help us develop these skills were discussed in the previous chapter.

Carry out a planned focus activity

The end goals of early learning are for children to become fluent speakers, skilled listeners, readers and writers, to be able to share and take turns, and be open to learn in many different ways. It is possible to plan the children's learning towards these general goals and to make provisions for them to achieve the specific early learning goals. However, planning should be carried out on a fairly short-term basis, not weeks, months or years in advance, as the most successful process by which young children learn is through self-chosen, self-directed play activities.

Adults who are active outdoors provide children with wonderful role models. If children only see bored, shivering adults outside they will model their behaviour on them and become bored themselves. They will show that they are bored by involving themselves in repetitious, uncooperative or stereotypical play. For example, when you see the same children racing around purposelessly on trikes or endlessly playing Batman, you know they are stuck for ideas. These children are not effective learners. The experience of taking part in planned activities helps children come up with interesting possibilities to try out on their own when their play is not being supported by adults.

Types of activity

Staff can choose from a whole range of daily activities. They might include:

- finding slugs;
- collecting or brushing up leaves;
- learning a new song about sliding down the slide;
- listening to the noise of a stick on different surfaces and tape recording the sounds;
- planting bulbs;

- weeding;
- taking part in outdoor imaginative play at the drive-through McDonald's made out of large cardboard boxes as part of a topic on food; or
- using the clipboards to count the number of lorries that pass by on the road outside the gate.

Many more examples of activities are give in Chapter 4.

Behind the content of each planned activity, there is a range of principles to bear in mind and also some aims and objectives that can be achieved.

Any planned activity should either be linked to something that a group or individual child has already been exploring, or introduce a new idea that is in some way connected with the children's interests. For instance, a herb-planting session could be planned for a group of children who have been exploring their love of sensory experiences. To ensure that activities build on and extend the children's own interests, the practitioner who is planning a day's activity needs to liaise with the practitioner who has been observing the children (in some settings, this may be the same person).

A well-planned activity will offer opportunities to extend children's learning in several areas of the curriculum at once. For example the herb garden mentioned above gives opportunities for:

- maths (counting, classifying, ordering and measuring);
- science (planting, watering, seeing the plants grow);
- language (descriptions of smells, colours, shapes, memories); and
- creative activities (using the herbs in real or pretend cooking, putting some leaves beside the easel to be incorporated into a painting).

All of these areas can be followed up on subsequent days.

The planned activity may have a follow-up activity that children can choose to take part in independently or explore for themselves. For example, if a planned activity is to plant bulbs, you could leave some plant pots, watering cans, marking sticks and pencils in the digging area when the planned activity is finished, so that children can play at planting bulbs on their own. Inside, make sure that there are books or a chart about planting bulbs and have a song, poem or story ready to teach at circle time on a related subject, for example: 'This is the way we plant our bulbs … when autumn comes along.'

An adult-led activity may focus on:

- skills training, for example throwing and catching balls, walking along a zigzag chalk-drawn line or consolidating other learning, such as playing: 'You can't cross the river' (see p. 80);

- real or maintenance work, such as gardening, cleaning the windows, washing the furniture or toys; or
- making something to play with which follows up on an observed interest, for example making kites inside and flying them outside.

A planned activity may last for just a few minutes or for much longer. When deciding on the length of time needed for any particular activity, consider:

- how many adults are available;
- how lively the children are; and
- how many new, young children there are.

At certain times of the year the planned activity may fit in with settling in new children, for example taking three new children on a tour of the outdoor area, however small it is. This would involve pointing out features, reinforcing rules positively or singing songs about putting things away.

If your area outside is sufficiently stimulating already, with lots of things for children to do independently, only a manageable number of children will want to do this planned activity with you. Alarm bells should ring about the quality of the rest of your provision if most of the children want to do what you are doing.

For details of how to plan an activity, see pp. 54–56 and the example planning sheet on pp. 62–63.

8 Writing a policy for outdoor play

One of the joys of early education is that practitioners work in teams of two or more people. Someone is always there to share a child's achievement or discuss a problem. However, a team also creates the potential for disagreement and confusion about the way forward, as within any group of practitioners there will be as many opinions on issues to do with children as there are members of staff. What we believe affects what we do and how we behave in practice. If there is a diversity of unheard or unspoken views, there may be inconsistency in the way that different members of staff interact with children. Priorities for the children may change, depending on who is making the decisions on a particular day, for example one practitioner was heard to say: 'We never go out when it is Jean's day to be here because she doesn't like outdoor play.'

A characteristic of full daycare and education is shift work, where sets of staff work early or late and where the time to plan together is limited. Another reality of early years education in pre-schools, playgroups, and day nurseries and centres can be the rapid turnover of staff. Under all these circumstances, consistency of philosophy and practice, and keeping everyone up to date can be difficult unless everything is written down.

It is not enough simply to write down what a setting wants to achieve, and why and how it will be achieved. Everyone needs to be involved in discussion about what is in the policy so that they feel part of the final agreement.

When new members of staff come they need to have a chance to understand what the policy means in the context of that particular setting, so a policy should be evaluated regularly so that it is kept relevant and completely up to date.

Ideally, the process of drawing up an outdoor play policy should involve parents and all the staff, including cleaners and kitchen staff. Everyone needs to be aware of the benefits of outdoor play, as children are very sensitive to all adults' views and chance remarks. A member of the kitchen staff at one setting was heard to joke with a child who was writing his name on the ground with some playground chalks that he would grow up to be a graffiti vandal, and it is possible that an unconscious expression such as this might have an adverse effect on the child's confidence.

Policy content

A policy for outdoor play needs to address the following issues, and could be organised under these headings:
1 Overall aims of outdoor play in our setting.
2 Planning and organisation of the outdoor environment (including how we meet the early learning goals).
3 Rules outside.
4 The role of adults outside.
5 Equality of opportunity outside, including statements about:
   - ensuring that all children whatever their ability are able to play and explore in the outdoor area;
   - boys' and girls' issues;
   - monitoring how children use the outdoor area;
   - equal presentation, eg tidying after the morning session to make sure that the afternoon session is equally well presented as a fresh area to explore; and
   - respect for cultural issues, eg some children may need to remain fully clothed even when the paddling pool is available.

Rules and safety for outside

As discussed in Chapter 2, even in a small space there is more room to move about outdoors than inside, so there is more opportunity for children to fall and bump themselves. Safety must therefore be at the heart of rules for the outdoors. Children have a self-preserving intelligence about keeping safe if they are allowed to use it, and the way to ensure that outdoor rules makes sense to children – and that they respect them – is to negotiate those rules not only with all members of staff but also with the children themselves.

One nursery asked a group of experienced children what would keep the new children from having accidents outside, and these 'experts' came up with an excellent set of rules:
- Don't push on the climbing frame.
- Don't climb up the slide.
- Don't go on the climbing frame when it is wet.
- Don't go on the bikes with dressing-up clothes on or they might get caught up in the wheels.
- Don't throw sand because it hurts your eyes.
- You must get off the bike when all the sand is through the timer.
- You mustn't hit or fight.
- You have to help to put everything away at tidy-up time.

The practitioner working with these children wrote all these rules down and then suggested that they could be turned round so that new children would know what to do, instead of what *not* to do. This shows how rules can be rephrased.

- We take care with sand – sand hurts if it gets in our eyes.
- We take care when we are on the climbing frame with others.
- We dry the climbing frame after rain, before climbing on it.
- We take turns on the bike.
- We climb up the steps before we go down the slide.
- We put things back in the trolley where we found them when it's time to tidy up.
- We hang up our dressing-up clothes before climbing or going on a wheeled toy.
- We are kind to our friends.

Staff then wrote out the rules on a large piece of coloured card, laminated it and displayed the rules outside for all to see.

When children don't like the rules

One staff group found they were always nagging certain children to put on their coats in cold weather. These children were not convinced that it was cold enough and moaned about putting on their coats or sneaked out without them on.

In response, practitioners developed an ingenious way to enforce the rule: 'You put your coat on when it is cold.'

The staff procured a large plaster pig and when they felt it was cold enough to wear coats, a blanket was put over the back of the pig. When the pig had its blanket on, coats had to be worn outside.

The staff didn't need to tell the children any more – the pig did all the wordless 'nagging' and, amazingly, there were no more arguments.

Dealing with uncooperative behaviour

Outside is a highly stimulating place for children and it is often the best place to learn many moral, spiritual and social lessons. But emotions run high when the play is engaged in seriously and, from time to time, they may spill into aggressive and uncooperative behaviour. It is sometimes hard for us to look on while children try to work out for themselves the dilemmas of fairness, sharing and becoming aware of the needs and feelings of others. Too often we hear the cries and step in quickly to save the situation from what we think will escalate. But with our intervention the stakes can become very high: children may give up and wait to have the situation resolved by the all-powerful 'teacher'; the 'offender' can be inadvertently shamed and the 'victim' glorified. Constant observation of the children will help to avoid this. It allows practitioners to see what is really going on so they are more likely to leave the children to try and resolve the situation themselves.

Such a situation is more difficult to handle when children hurt each other. However, the whole approach to an outdoor area can help to reduce the chance of this happening, as research has indicated that levels of aggression in young children are low especially when:

- staff are fully trained in early childhood education;
- staff join children in their play and have challenging conversations with them;
- there is easy and free access between inside and outside; and
- children can explore an interesting environment.[41]

It is important to include sanctions for breaking the rules in the outdoor play policy so that there is a consistency of action, and all staff members need to decide how to deal with aggression outside. In one nursery, the sanctions for unacceptable behaviour are:

1 The child is given a verbal warning with a reminder of the rule and an explanation. If the unacceptable behaviour persists, then:

2 The child is sent inside for five to ten minutes. If the unacceptable behaviour still persists, then:

3 The child is sent inside for the remainder of the session.

A policy on outdoor behaviour means that staff will help children to manage their behaviour in a consistent way. Everyone – children, staff and parents – will be involved in drawing up guidelines.

9 Parents and carers

Parents are the people from whom young children learn the most. What parents value, children value, and so it is crucial to make sure that parents see the benefits of outdoor provision for their child.

Understandably, the emphasis on play in the early years curriculum can be very confusing for parents as, in general English usage, the term 'play' tends to be used as the opposite of 'work' and even of 'learning'. So the inclusion of outdoor play as an integral part of a session and not just a 15-minute break can lead to serious misunderstandings. What the practitioner values might be at odds with the perceptions and memory of the parents' own school days. A parent said to me: 'Playtime, in school as I remember it, was a release from learning, but these children seem to have playtime all the time.' Clearly, this parent concludes that the children are not learning when they are outside.

Parents can be very puzzled about the reasons for sand and water play or the need and even desirability for their child to be messy or apparently 'purposeless' at nursery.

Nursery settings that encourage outdoor exploration implicitly believe that a certain amount of dirtiness and disorder is desirable or at least acceptable in children:

> that imagination and creativity are important goals and that reading for pleasure is self-evidently desirable. But parents who put a high value on hard work, cleanliness, obedience and gaining skills may not warm to the sight of their children splashing in the water tray, or feel enthusiastic about their 'creations' – which look to them like scribbles or daubs of paint. They might prefer to see their children settling down, 'concentrating' or producing a line of carefully traced writing.[42]

Children may spend all the glorious day in the outdoor environment happily making sense of their world with their friends, but if they even sense a parent's negative comments about wasted time out of doors they can become confused. A tension is set up that, by playing out of doors, children might not be pleasing their parents, and that can be very upsetting for them. Who, for instance, has not heard a child say: 'My mum doesn't want me to play outside, because she says I'll get dirty'? This kind of parental view is steeped in social attitudes about what constitutes 'learning'. But while negative parental attitudes to outdoor play may have complex roots, it is important that we do not use them as a reason to stay indoors. Instead, it is our professional responsibility to explain the benefit of outdoor play.

Sharing the importance of the outdoor curriculum with parents

The process of establishing a partnership with parents, where practitioners and parents understand each other, consists of long- and short-term strategies. There is no 'quick fix'. Perhaps the greatest challenge and benefit to practitioners is to become skilful at informing and explaining to parents in accessible language about some quite complex ideas. Parents need to understand:

■ the many reasons why outdoor play is so important (see Chapter 1); and

■ the ways in which outdoor provision supports the development of their child and the early learning goals.

In presenting this information to parents, it is very important that practitioners know:

■ how to listen to parents;

■ what parents expect their child to learn;

■ as much as possible about their child; and

■ how to inform parents about the importance of outdoor play as a means of effective learning.

Involving parents in the outdoor area is one of the best ways to help them appreciate its benefits. When a setting keeps parents informed about developments in their garden or outdoor area, they can be enlisted to help in fundraising and even digging, weeding, general maintenance and playing with the children outside. Some settings that

How one setting presents its outdoor policy to parents

'At the initial meeting with parents and carers we flag up very clearly that children need space and an outdoor environment in order to learn. We show parents our outdoor area and describe what the children learn there. We also inform them that their children will probably want to be out in all weathers and will need to be dressed appropriately. We back up this information with a video and an attractive and instructive photographic display.

When we put up a display about anything, for instance how we teach number, we always make sure there are plenty of photos featuring the outdoor environment. We keep a record in photographic albums of the developments in the outdoor environment.

We have had a parents' evening for parents who work, to show them round the garden, and we run a competition for them with challenges about maths and science – things like how many insects they can see and name.

Parents know it is an important area because most of the stories children recount to them are about the good times they've had during the day in the garden.'

do not have direct access to an outdoor area have enlisted parents on a rota basis as extra adults to accompany children in and out.

As a final note to this issue, here are some of the notices that were displayed in the Rachel McMillan Nursery School when I was head teacher. These sought to inform parents about the school's overall policy on the outdoors and on the specific learning that can happen outside. They were part of our open dialogue with parents, to create positive attitudes among the vast majority who placed their children in the school – and can be adapted to suit any setting.

Margaret McMillan, our founder, said that children need space as much as they need food and air, in order to grow. The wonderful garden here ensures that city children now, as in the past, can feel life in every limb. There are corners and steps to manoeuvre when riding a tricycle or pushing a truck; there are places to hide, triggering the imagination. Ponds, mini-beasts, plants and trees become part of children's play experience as they explore their world and build friendships.

We believe so strongly that children learn through playing in large stimulating spaces, that the outdoor area is available to the children ALL DAY. Of course this means that we have to plan the outdoor area very carefully so that we are offering all experiences necessary for educational development. By monitoring the children and ourselves and by involving you, the parents, we make sure that each child is making the most of their nursery school experience.

Language and literacy

When children look into the pond to find snails or tadpoles, it excites their curiosity and encourages them to express their wonder about living things. The outdoor environment motivates children to 'act out' stories using language creatively. Seeing a spider may inspire the child to think or dramatise about the 'Anansi and the Alligator' story. Children have access to chalks and can write or draw in a big way on the ground or on the walls. Often, words which are meaningful in a particular part of the garden or for a particular activity, such as 'Start here', 'Jump down' or 'Stop!', will be written by staff or children.

Mathematical development

Maths is not just about learning numbers. It is much more. Through their play with each other and with staff, children are building up concepts about size, shape, pattern and order. Ideas about more and less, short and tall are tested, and problems are solved alone or with the help of others. The equipment and the environment itself are so enticing that children want to find out *why* the pram can't get through that small space.

Mathematical language, so essential for consolidating ideas, is being used all the time, for instance: 'Look at me I'm higher than you' (shouted from the climbing frame); 'I got here first' ; bigger, longer, faster, more or less – all are used in the right context to be understood. Children using boxes and blocks to build a house or a boat are at the same time exploring geometric shapes and basic physics when getting their structure to stand up.

Social and emotional development

In the garden, there are areas where children can be alone, quietly coming to terms with their own thoughts, while looking on at the play of others. At the same time the equipment we provide encourages children to play cooperatively and to value each other's contribution; pushing someone on the swing or taking turns on the slide.

We seek to extend the children's experiences outside our gate by taking small groups to post a letter, looking at a digger in action, discovering the River Thames and generally observing people at work, like the firefighter or the doctor in her clinic.

Scientific experiences

Exploring, investigating, observing are the cornerstones of understanding. In the garden is a large variety of animal and plant life which children are looking at. The tadpole–frog life cycle, the snail trail, worms and spider webs are gleefully discovered, and curiosity is awakened and satisfied. While digging and planting children are exploring the constituents of soil and how the weather affects it – it's hard to dig after a frost. Forces are investigated – it's easier to pull the cart up the hill when it's empty but when it's full you may need help. A pulley or lever is fun to use if you want to lift heavy things.

Playing with tubes where sound is amplified over a distance is fascinating to young children, along with all the other ways that sound can be explored out of doors. Children can shout or roar like a lion and the xylophone sounds different when played inside a barrel.

Physical development

Children learn through their whole bodies. The exciting equipment and the way in which the staff arrange it encourage the children to test their physical powers to the full. They run faster, lift things that are heavier, are motivated to hit a ball with a bat (conveniently tied to elastic so that it always comes back), all of which help to develop hand–eye coordination. Large and small muscles are exercised, and the children's faces express satisfaction and achievement which exertion gives them.

Accidents are few because children soon develop an awareness of their own capabilities and they set their own safety limits. However staff are always vigilant, helping children to reach new goals today which tomorrow they will improve on.

Notes

1   McMillan, M. (1919) *The nursery school*, Dent, p. 50.
2   McMillan, M. (1927) *The life of Rachel McMillan*, p. 40.
3   McMillan, M. (c. 1925) *Nursery schools and the pre-school child*, NSA Publication.
4   Ouvry, M. (1992) 'The McMillan legacy', unpublished MA dissertation, University of London.
5   QCA (2000) *Curriculum guidance for the foundation stage*, Qualifications and Curriculum Authority, p. 25.
6   Bateson, P. (1999) 'Let children play', *The Guardian*, 8 September.
7   Early Childhood Education Forum (1998) *Quality in diversity in early learning: a framework for early childhood practitioners*, National Children's Bureau, p. 37.
8   Kipling, R. (1903) *Just so stories*.
9   Sutcliffe *et al.* (1987) 'Learning to move and moving to learn in the nursery years', *British Journal of Physical Education*, vol. 18, no. 4.
10 Cooper, K. H. (1987) Public lecture in Newcastle-upon-Tyne. In *Journal of physical education*, vol. 18, no.5.
11 Sports Council (1988) *Sport and young people*.
12 McMillan, M. (1930), *The nursery school*, Dent, p. 23.
13 Lindon, J. (1999) *Too safe for their own good?* National Early Years Network.
14 Berk, L. E. & Winsler, A. (1995) *Scaffolding children's learning: Vygotsky and early childhood education*, National Association for the Education of Young Children, Washington: DC, p. 97.
15 Bilton, H. (1998) *Outdoor play in the early years: management and innovation*, David Fulton.
16 Finch, S. (1999) quoted by J. Moorhead in 'Out of the mouths of babes', *The Guardian*, 2 June.
17 Bruce, T. (1989) *Early childhood education*, Hodder & Stoughton, p. 55.
18 Goddard Blythe, S. (2000) 'First steps to the most important ABC', *Times Educational Supplement*, 7 January.
19 Ragsdale G., in Nuttall, W. (1999) 'The effects of posture on learning', *Early years*, vol. 20, no. 1.
20 Lasenby, M. (1990) *The early years – a curriculum for young children: outdoor play*, Harcourt Brace Jovanovich.
21 Wylie, C. (1996) *Five years old and competent*, New Zealand Curriculum Education Research; Bredekamp, S. & Copple, C. (1997) *Developmentally appropriate practice in early childhood programs*, National Association for the Education of Young Children, available from the National Early Years Network; Ball, C. (1994) *Start right: the importance of early learning*, Royal Society of Arts, p. 55, para. 6.9.
22 Community Playthings, Robertsbridge, East Sussex, TN32 5DR.
23 More information about setting up a kitchen garden can be found in Buck, L. (1999) 'Acting naturally – the outdoor environment', *Early years educator*, vol. 1, no. 2, June.
24 For example NES Arnold, Kent Educational Supplies and Community Playthings.
25 Sutcliffe *et al.* (1987) 'Learning to move and moving to learn in the nursery years', *British journal of physical education*, vol. 18, no. 4, p. 157.

26 Sutcliffe *et al.* (1987) 'Learning to move and moving to learn in the nursery years', *British journal of physical education*, vol. 18, no. 4.

27 Gallahue, D. L. (1982) *Understanding motor development in children*, New York, Wiley.

28 For a list of developmental stages, see Hobart, C. & Frankel, J. (1994) *A practical guide to child observation*, Stanley Thornes, pp. 115–119.

29 More information about schemas can be found in Nutbrown, K. (1994) *Threads of thinking*, Paul Chapman Publishing; & Athey, C. (1990) *Extending thought in young children*, Paul Chapman Publishing.

30 For more information about 'gun play' see Holland, P. (1999) 'Is zero tolerance intolerance?', *Early childhood practice*, vol. 1, no. 1.

31 QCA (2000) *Curriculum guidance for the foundation stage*, Qualifications and Curriculum Authority.

32 Hall, L. (1998) 'Children's self-assessment', Clyde Nursery School, London.

33 Other teaching techniques can be found in McNaughton, G. & Williams, G. (1999) *Techniques for teaching young children: choices in theory and practice*, Longman.

34 Hutchin, V. (1996) *Tracking significant achievement*, Hodder & Stoughton.

35 Ditto, p. 57.

36 Adapted from Lally, M. & Hurst, V. (1991), quoted in *Great expectations* (Westminster Curriculum for Under-fives), p. 6.27.

37 Browne, E. (1995) *Handa's surprise*, Walker Books.

38 Hewitt, A. (1994) *Mrs Mopple's washing line*, Red Fox.

39 Browne, E. (1995) *Handa's surprise*, Walker Books.

40 From Buck, L., 'The Pound Park experience – a seasonal diary of environmental education in the early years', Pound Park Nursery School, Charlton Lane, London SE7 3EH.

41 Wylie, C (1996) *Five years old and competent*, New Zealand Curriculum Education Research.

42 Tizard, B., Mortimore, J. & Burchell, B. (1981) *Involving parents in nursery and infant schools*, Grant McIntyre, p. 63.